Alfred's Premier Piano Course

Gayle Kowalchyk • E. L. Lancaster

Notespeller 1A is designed to be used with Lesson Book 1A of *Alfred's Premier Piano Course.* It can also serve as an effective supplement for other piano methods.

Notespeller 1A reinforces note-reading concepts presented in the Lesson Book through written exercises. Note and interval identification exercises are presented to provide systematic reinforcement to help the student read and write notes on the staff.

The pages in this book correlate page by page with the materials in Lesson Book 1A. They should be assigned according to the instructions in the upper right corner of pages in this book. They also may be assigned as review material at any time after the student has passed the designated Lesson Book page.

In addition to written exercises, unique features of the book include:

- Short explanations of musical concepts to use as a review before completing the written activities.
- Reinforcement of the rhythm patterns introduced in Lesson 1A.
- Note-reading exercises that introduce the student to famous composers.
- Colorful illustrations that relate to the art used in Lesson 1A.

Look for QR codes (▦) throughout the book.

1. Download a free QR code app to a smart phone from iTunes® or Google Play™.
2. Open the app, and then hold the smart phone above the QR code.

Within seconds, a Premier Online Assistant video corresponding to the page in this book will play. These videos provide additional explanations of concepts.

Illustrations by Jimmy Holder

ISBN-10: 1-4706-1487-1
ISBN-13: 978-1-4706-1487-4

Use with Alfred's Premier Piano Course, Lesson Book 1A, page 18

The Music Alphabet

The white keys on the piano are named using the first seven letters of the alphabet.

A B C D E F G

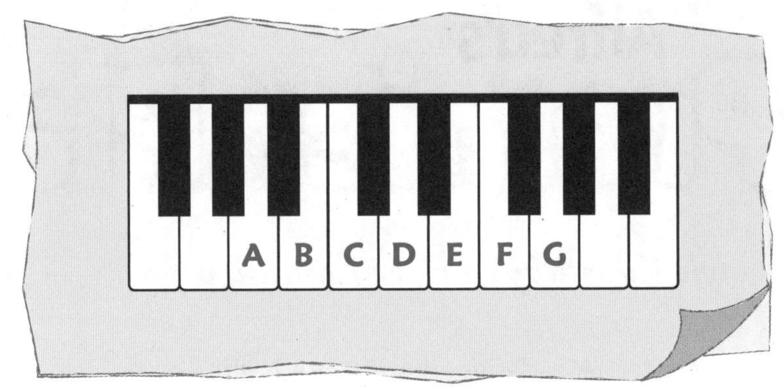

1. Write the music alphabet on the blank lines.

2. Write the missing letter names from the music alphabet on the blank lines.

3. Write the music alphabet two times on the white keys.

4. Climb the ladder by writing the music alphabet going up.

Lesson Book: page 19

C–D–E on the Keyboard

- **C** is the white key to the *left* of two black keys.
- **D** is the white key *between* two black keys.
- **E** is the white key to the *right* of two black keys.

1. Write the letter name on each key marked X.

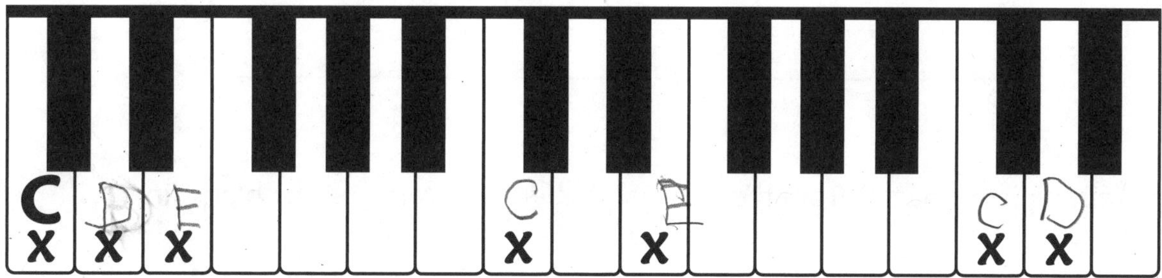

2. Draw a line to connect each key marked X to its correct anchor.

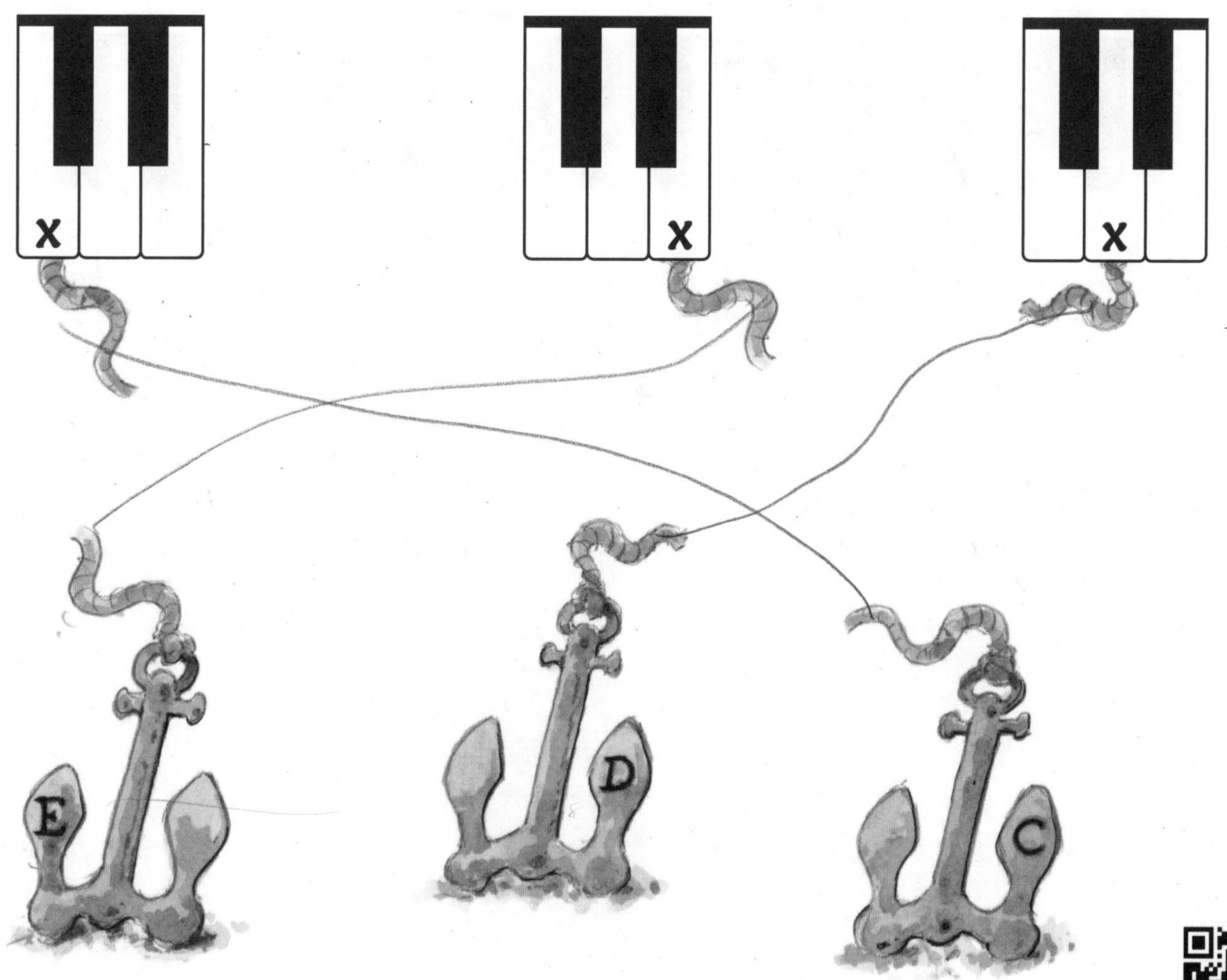

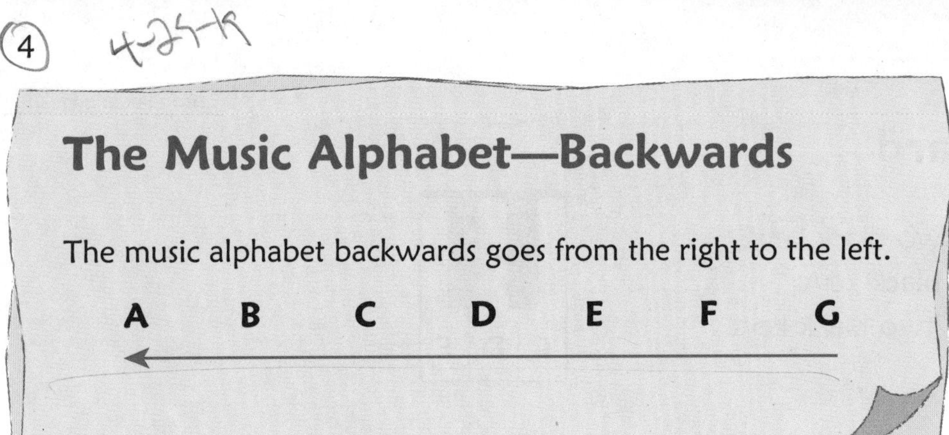

The Music Alphabet—Backwards

The music alphabet backwards goes from the right to the left.

A B C D E F G

1. Write the music alphabet backwards on the blank lines.

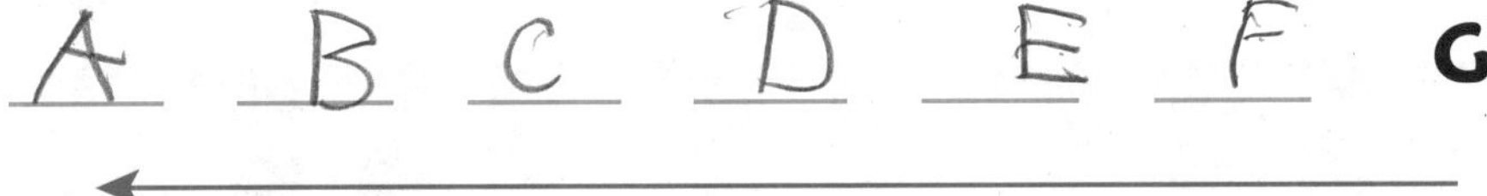

2. Write the missing letter names from the music alphabet backwards on the blank lines.

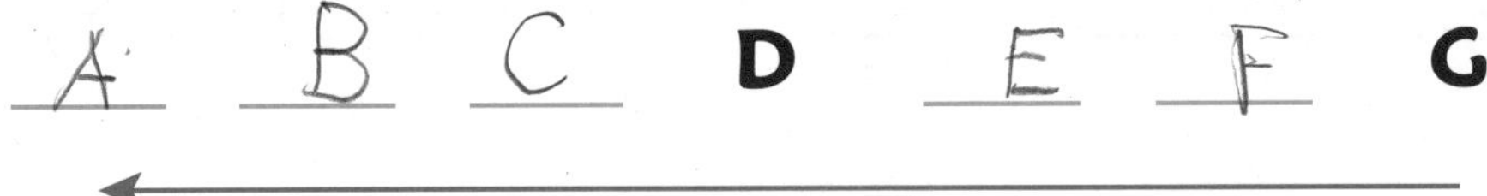

3. Write the music alphabet backwards two times on the white keys.

4. Go down the stairs by writing the music alphabet backwards.

Lesson Book: pages 22–23

G and A on the Keyboard

- **G** is the white key to the *left* of the black key in the middle of the three-black-key group.
- **A** is the white key to the *right* of the black key in the middle of the three-black-key group.

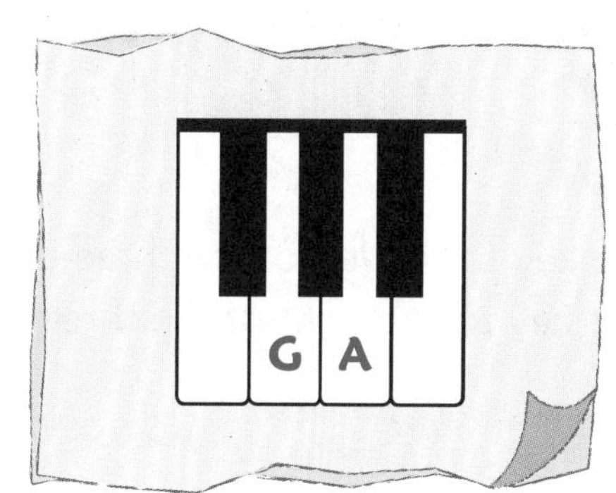

Draw a computer cord to connect the letter name on each mouse to its matching key on the computer screen.

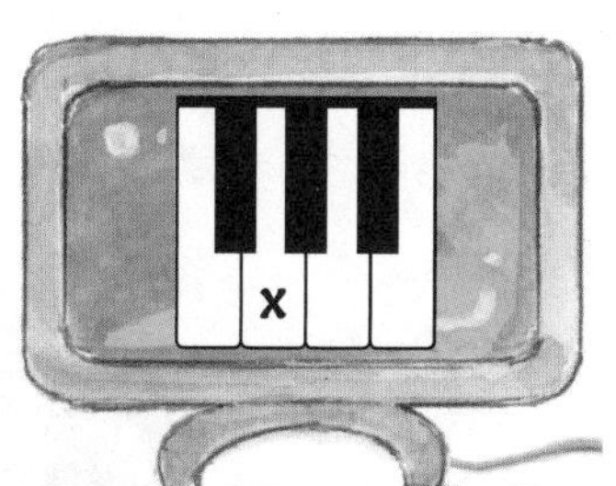

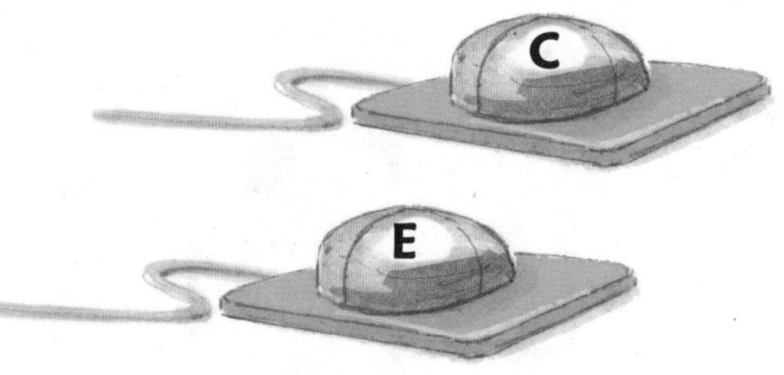

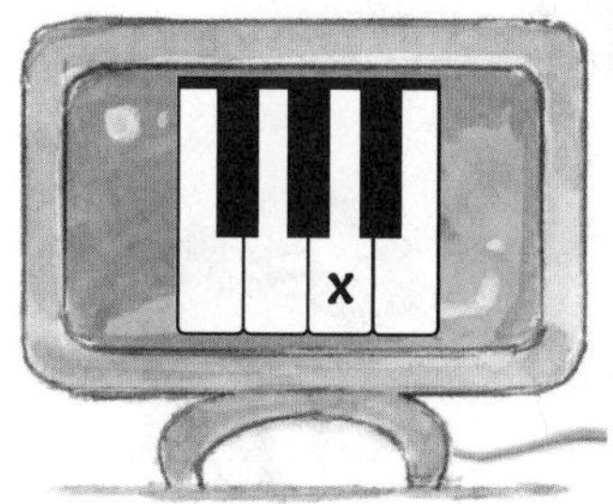

Lesson Book: pages 24–25

F and B on the Keyboard

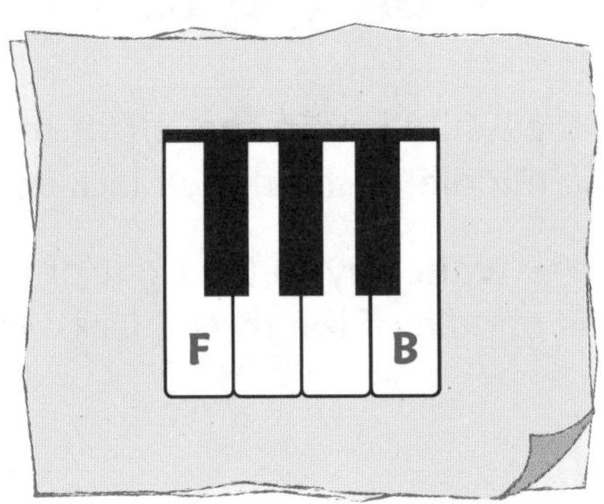

- **F** is the white key to the *left* of the three-black-key group.
- **B** is the white key to the *right* of the three-black-key group.

Draw a line to connect the letter name on each helmet to its matching key on the rock wall.

B

A

G

F

C

Lesson Book: page 26

Step

A step moves up or down to the:

- next **key**.
- next **finger**.
- next **letter**.

1. Write the letter names that are *up* and *down* a step from each given letter.

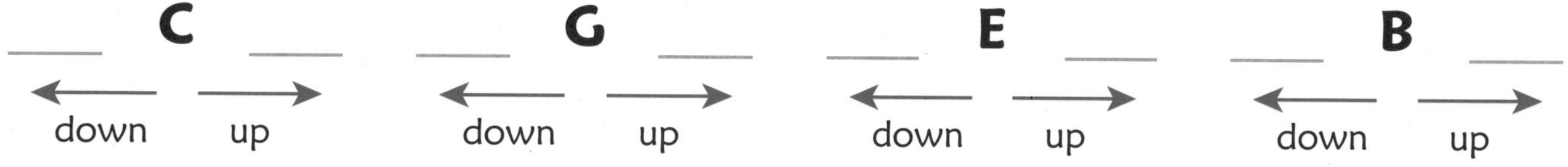

2. Write the number above the finger that is *up* a step from each given finger number.

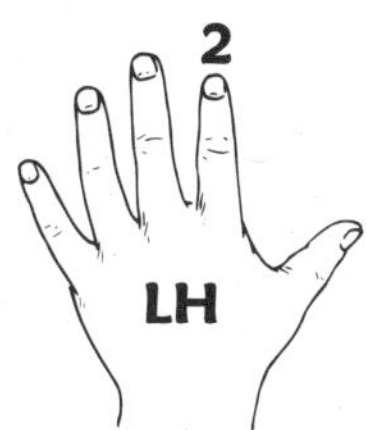

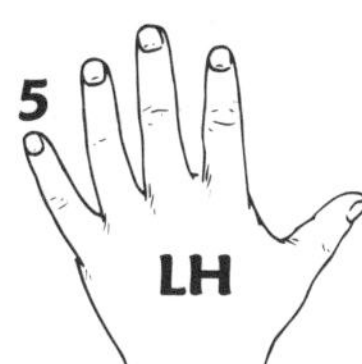

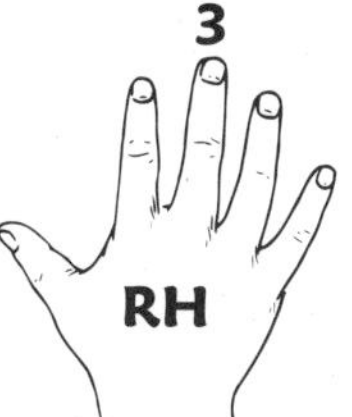

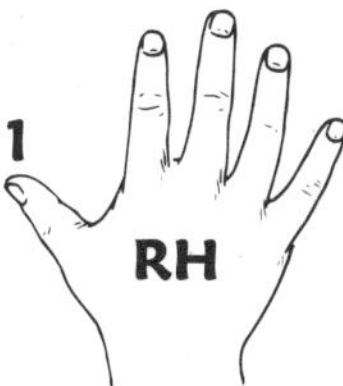

3. Write the number above the finger that is *down* a step from each given finger number.

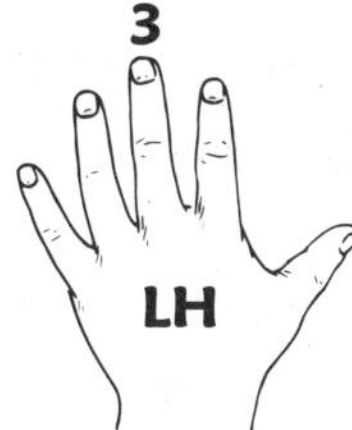

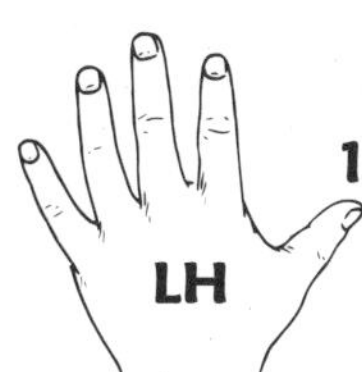

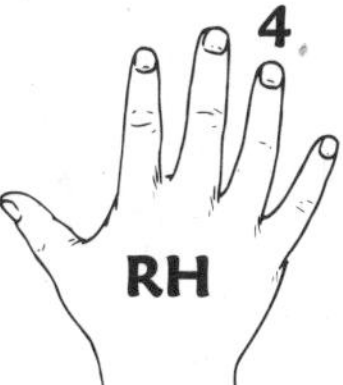

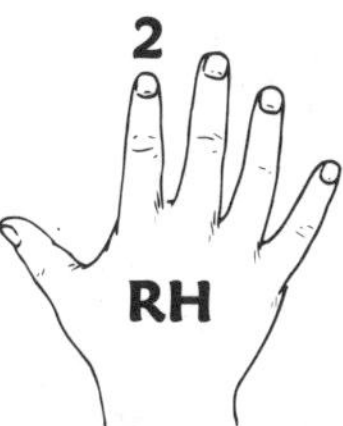

4. Write the letter name on the key that is *up* a step from each key marked X.

5. Write the letter name on the key that is *down* a step from each key marked X.

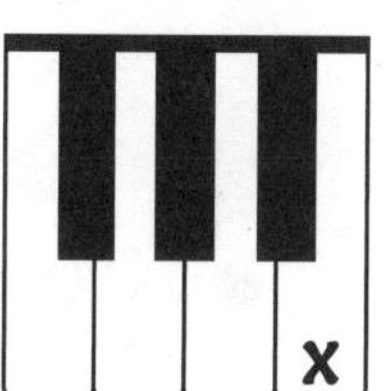

Lesson Book: page 28

Steps in Rhythm

1. Write steps going *up* below each rhythm pattern.
   Then, using RH finger 3 on each key, play on the keyboard.

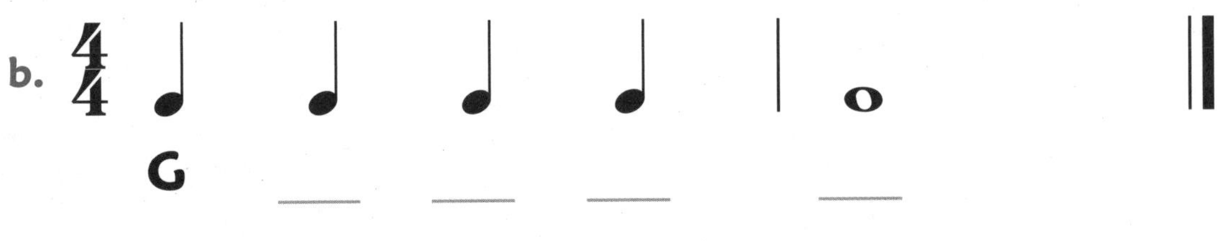

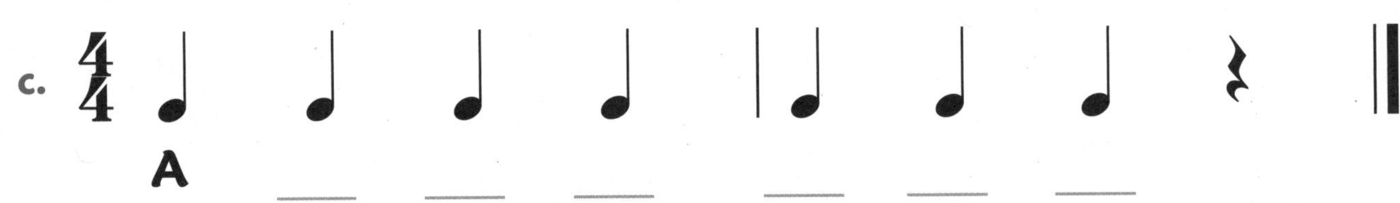

2. Write steps going *down* below each rhythm pattern.
   Then, using LH finger 3 on each key, play on the keyboard.

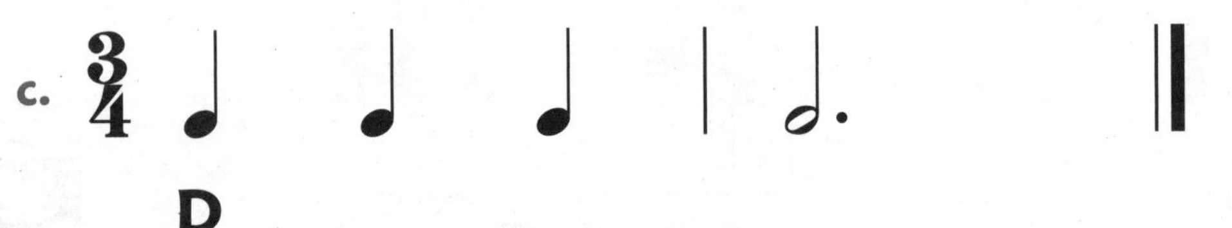

Lesson Book: page 29

Middle C and Bass C

Bass C is one **octave** (8 notes) lower than Middle C.

Draw a line to connect the key marked X on each keyboard to its name beside Big Ben.

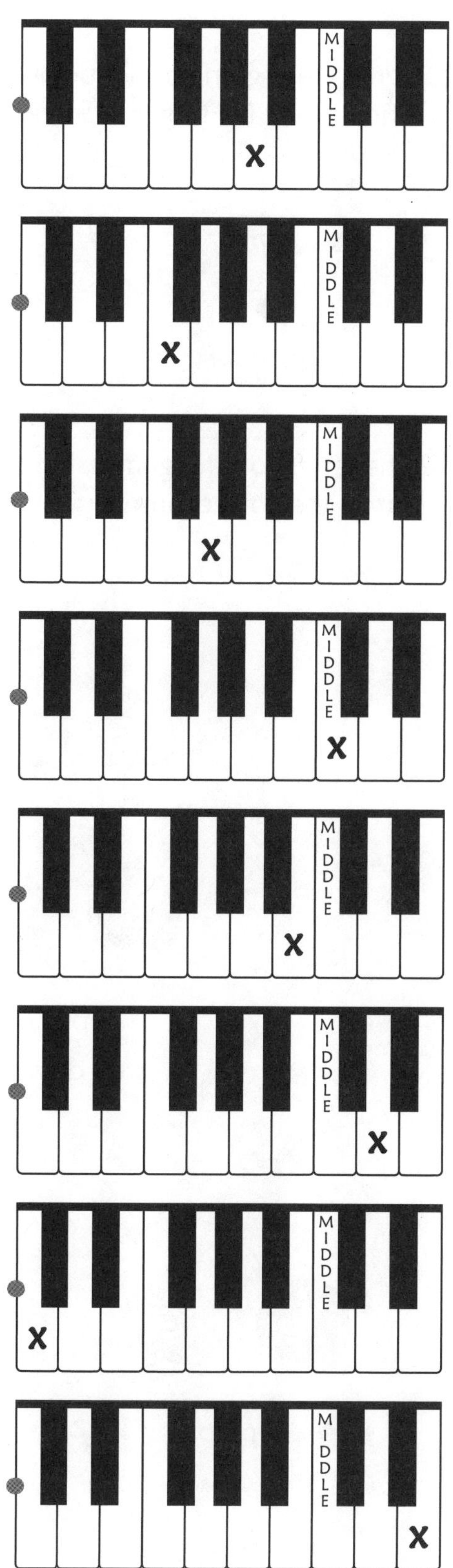

Lesson Book: page 30

More Steps

1. Write steps going *up* below each rhythm pattern.
   Then, using RH finger 3 on each key, play on the keyboard.

2. Write steps going *down* below each rhythm pattern.
   Then, using LH finger 3 on each key, play on the keyboard.

3. The letters on the gum balls show a step *up* or *down* on the keyboard.
   Circle the correct answer.

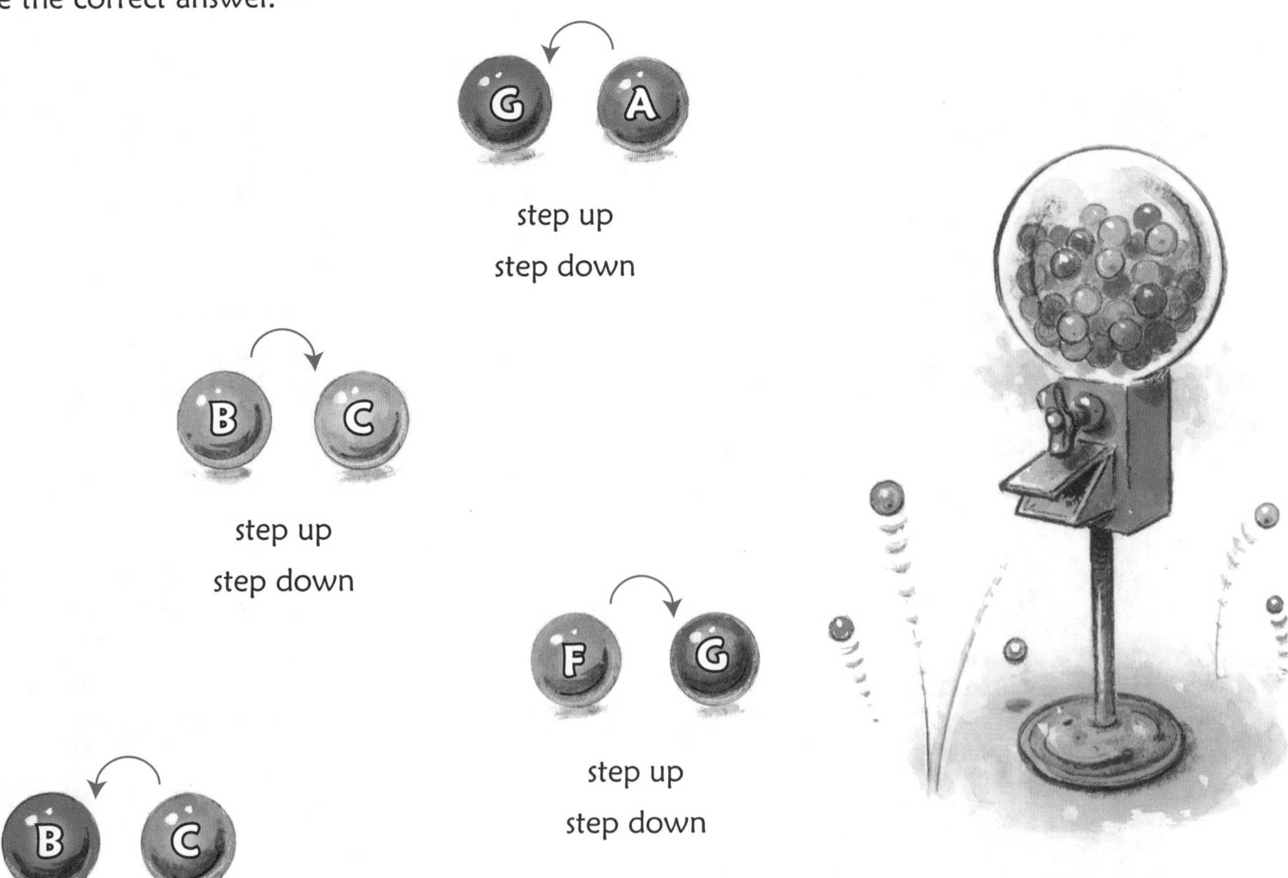

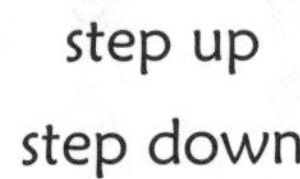

Lesson Book: page 32

The Staff

Music is written on the 5 lines and 4 spaces of the staff.

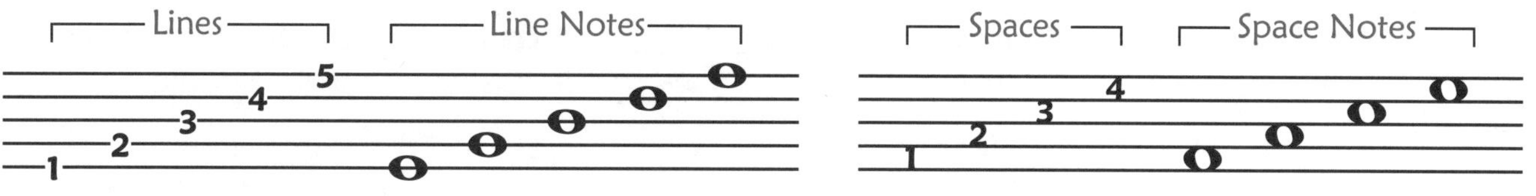

1. Number the *lines* on the staff.

2. Number the *spaces* on the staff.

3. Draw a whole note *on* each numbered line and *in* each numbered space.

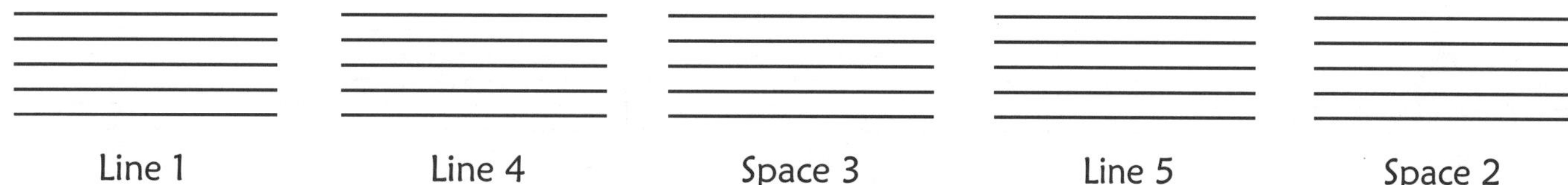

4. Draw a line to connect the notes on the left to the escalators moving in the same direction.

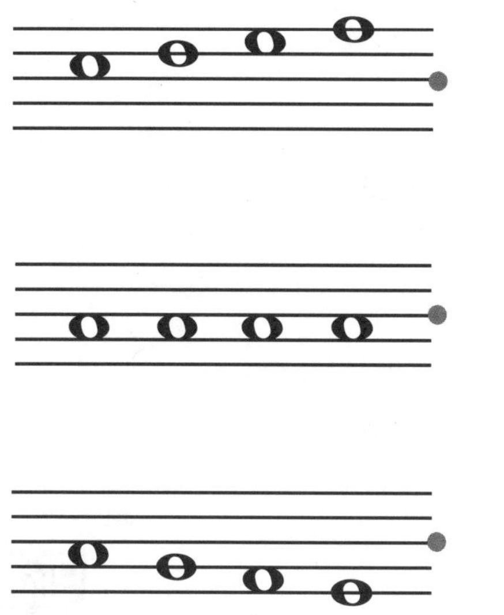

Lesson Book: page 33

Bass Clef and Treble Clef

A **bass clef** on the staff usually shows notes *below* Middle C.

Notes on the bass clef staff are usually played by the *left* hand.

A **treble clef** on the staff usually shows notes *above* Middle C.

Notes on the treble clef staff are usually played by the *right* hand.

1. Draw four treble clef signs.

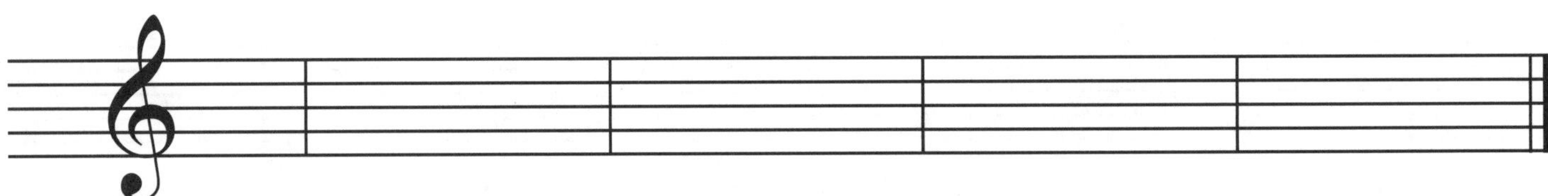

2. Draw four bass clef signs.

3. Circle the hand that usually plays notes in the treble clef.

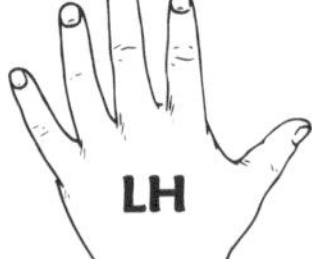

4. Circle the hand that usually plays notes in the bass clef.

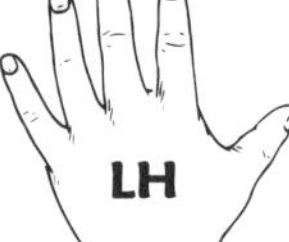

Lesson Book: page 34

The Grand Staff and Middle C

The *treble staff* and the *bass staff* are joined together with a *brace* and a *bar line* to make a *grand staff.*

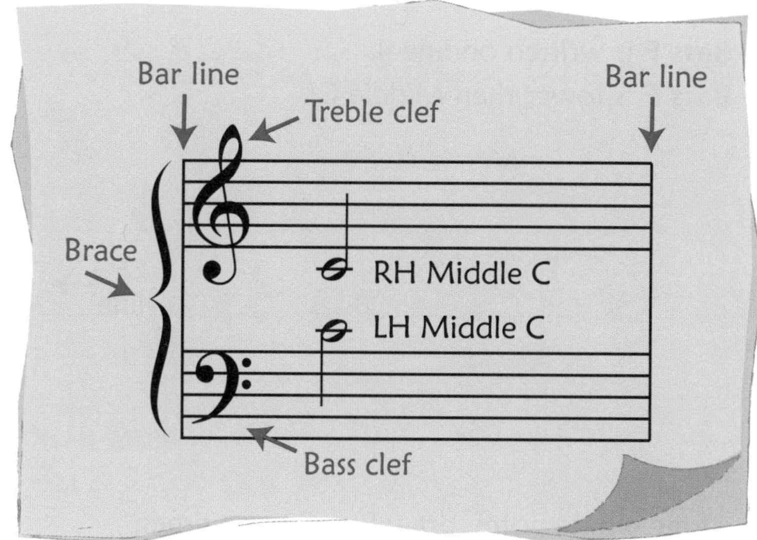

1. Draw two grand staffs by following these steps:
   - Draw a treble clef sign on the top staff.
   - Draw a bass clef sign on the bottom staff.
   - Draw a bar line at the beginning and end of the two staffs.
   - Draw a brace at the beginning of the two staffs.

2. On the blank lines, write RH if the Middle C is played by the right hand. Write LH if the Middle C is played by the left hand.

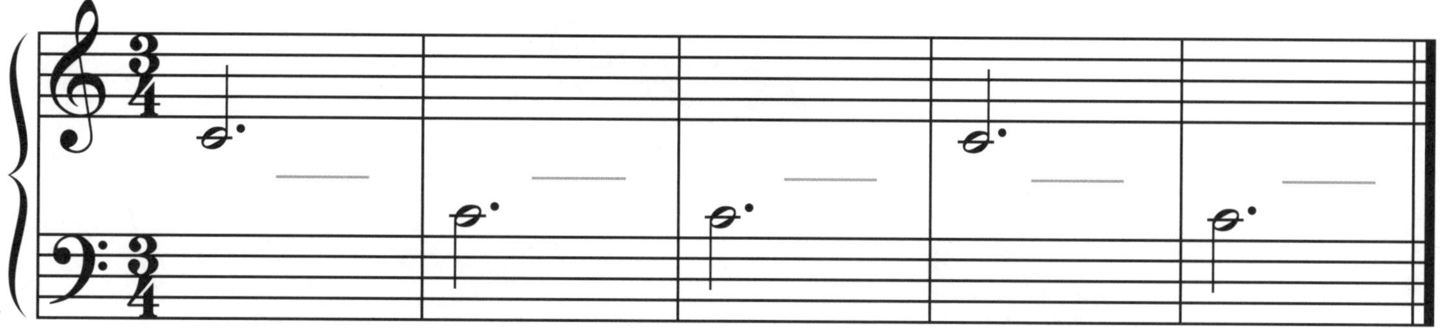

Lesson Book: page 36

Bass F and Middle C

- **Bass F** is written on line 4.
- **Bass F** is lower than Middle C.

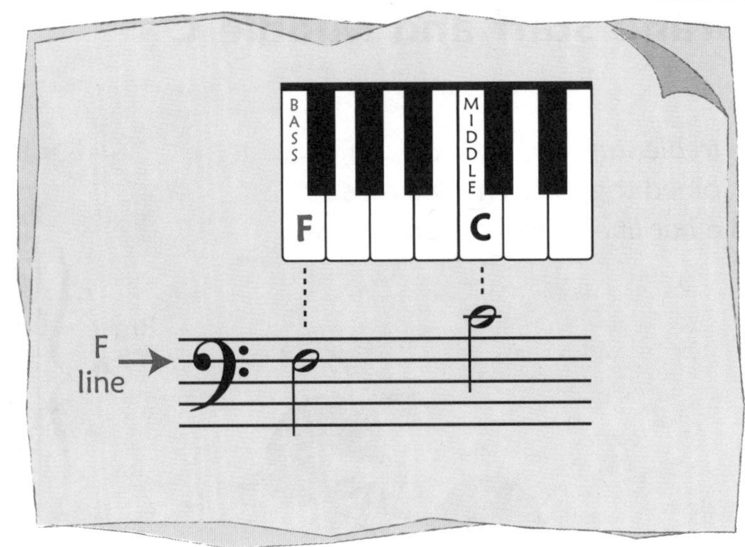

1. Using whole notes, draw Bass F three times.

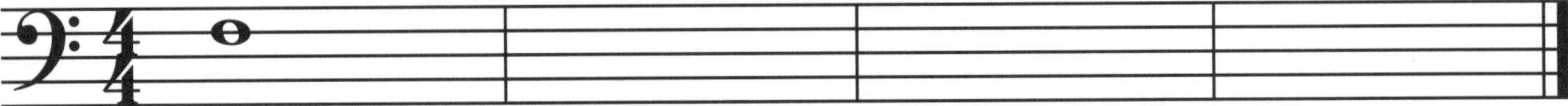

2. Using whole notes, draw Middle C in bass clef three times.

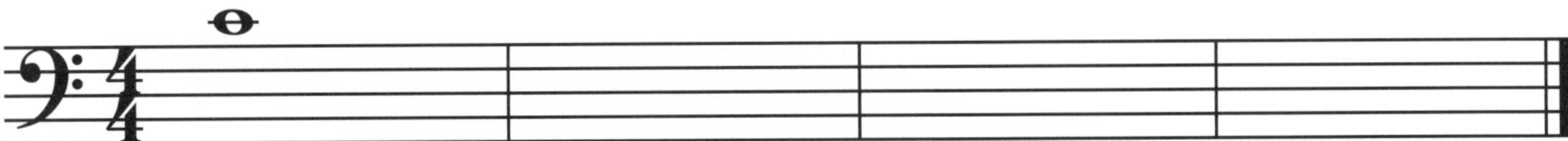

3. Circle each arrowhead that contains a Bass F.

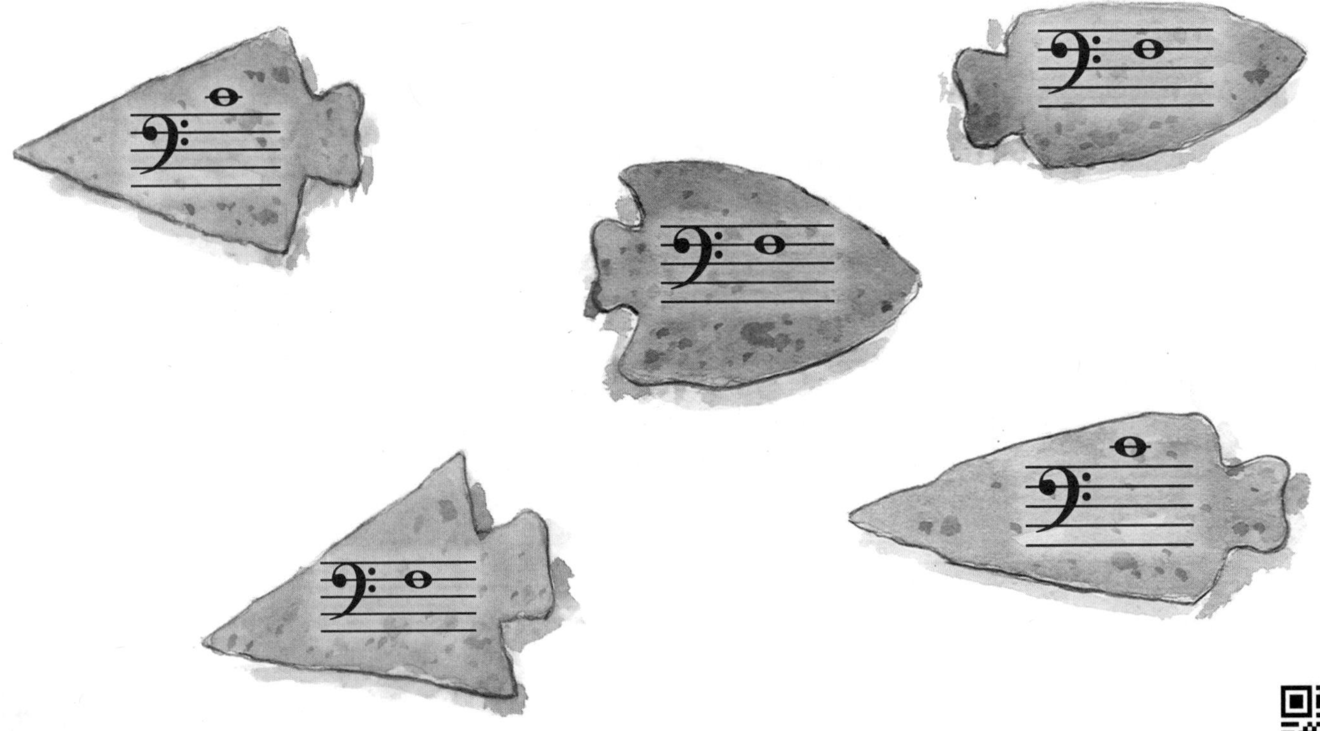

Lesson Book: page 39

Treble G

- **Treble G** is written on line 2.
- **Treble G** is higher than Middle C.

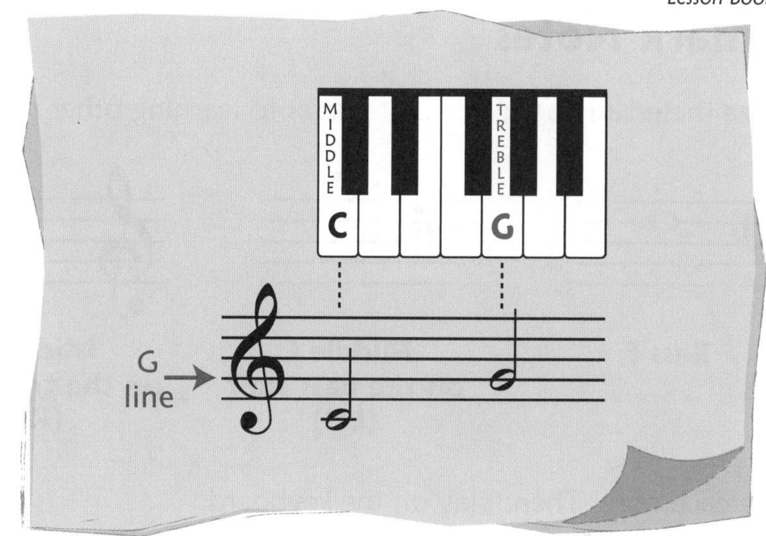

1. Using whole notes, draw Treble G three times.

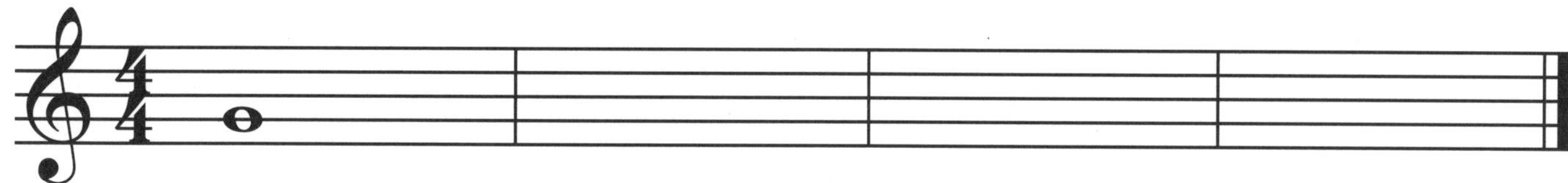

2. Circle each aspen leaf that contains a Treble G.

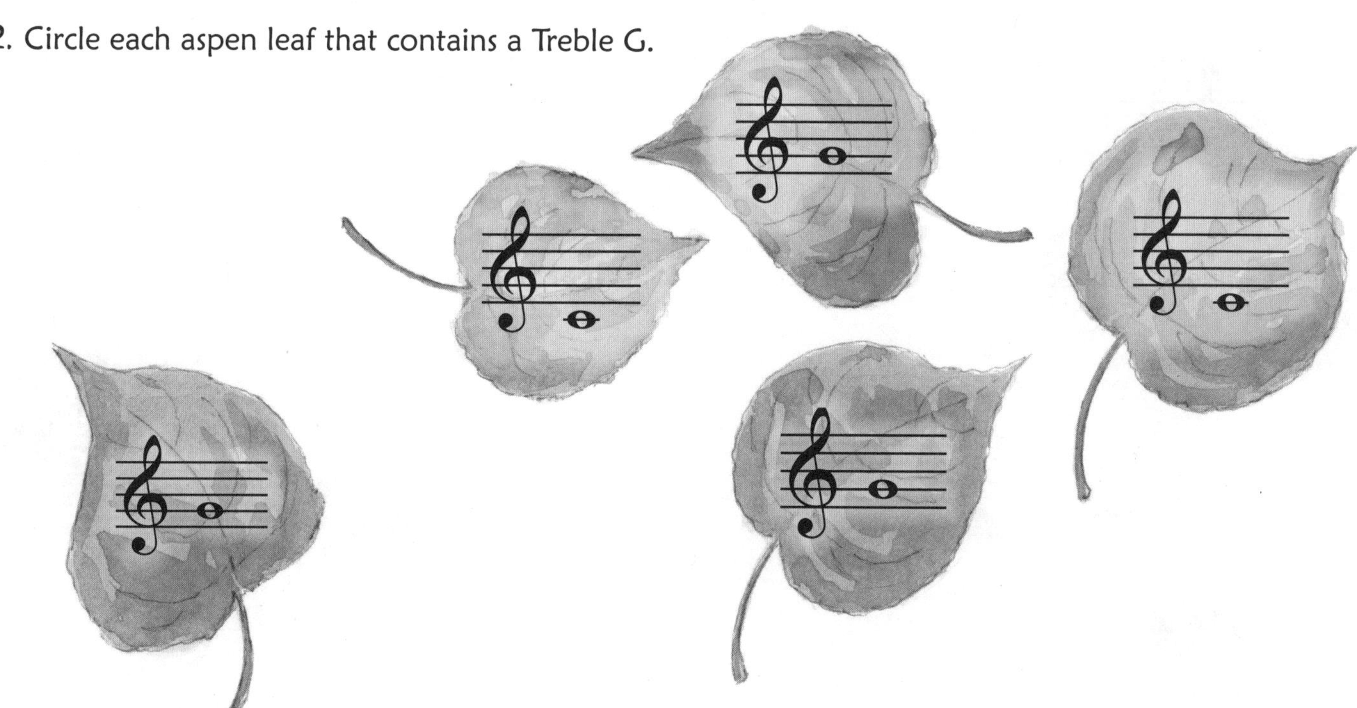

3. Write the letter F on Bass F.

4. Write the letter G on Treble G.

Lesson Book: page 41

Landmark Notes

Memorize these Landmark Notes as guides to learning other notes.

1. Name each note. Then, play on the keyboard.

2. Draw a line to connect each note on a spaceship to its matching name on one of the planets.

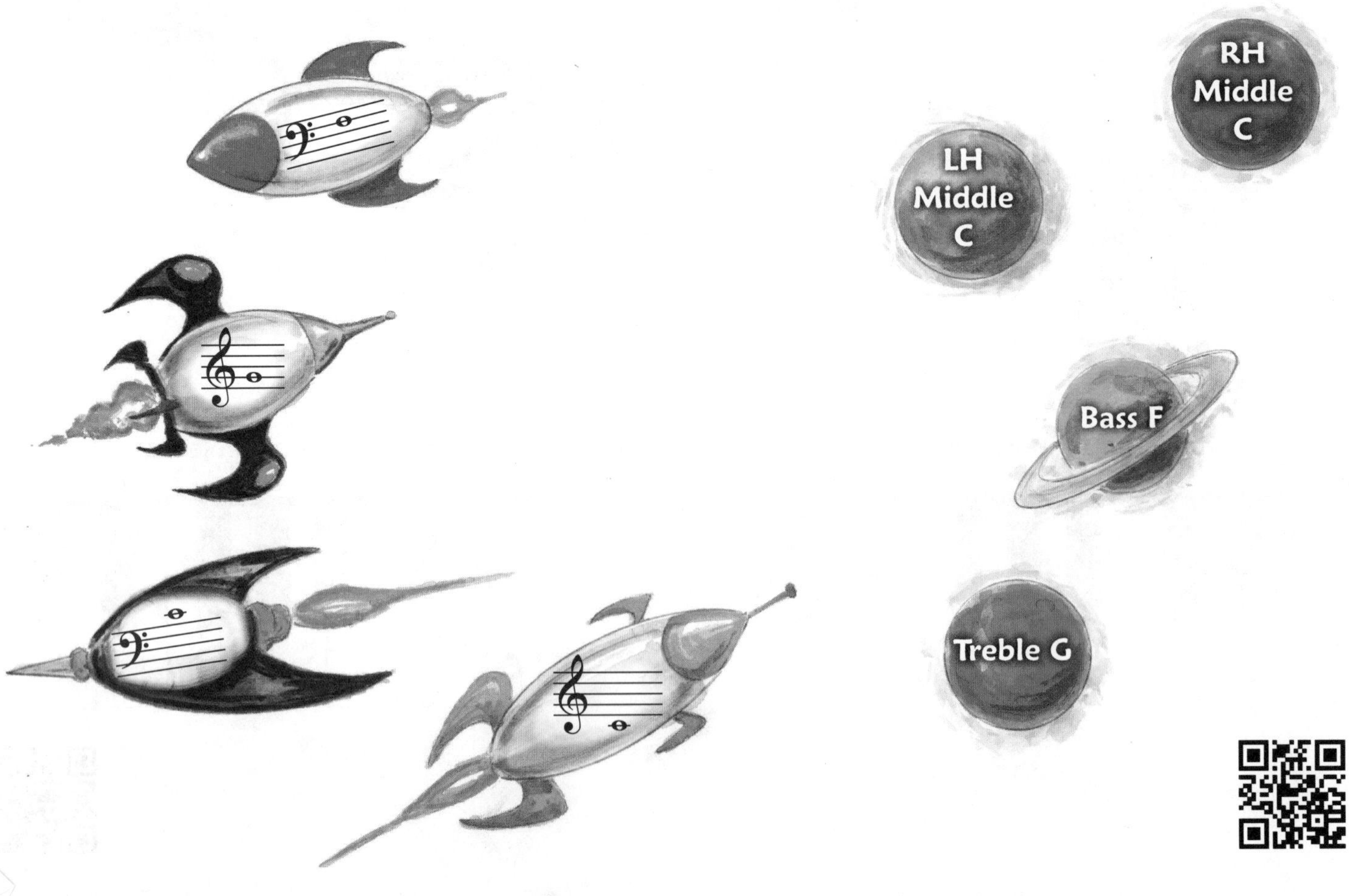

RH Middle C

LH Middle C

Bass F

Treble G

Lesson Book: page 42

Steps on the Staff

On the staff, a step moves *up* or *down* to the next line or space.

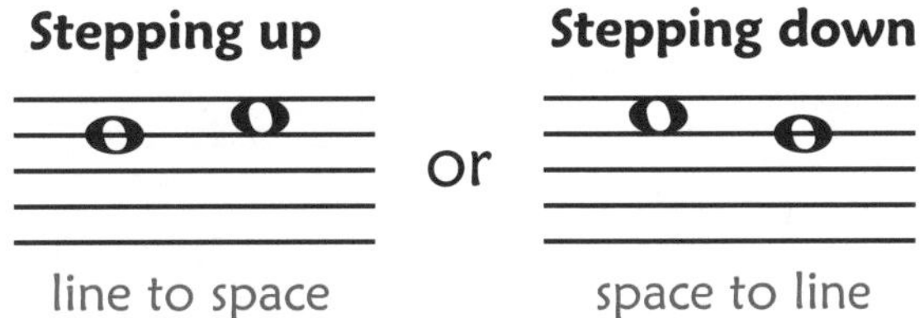

1. Draw a line to connect each *step* on the staff to the ice skate that describes how it moves.

- **Bass G** is a step *up* from Bass F.
- **Bass G** is written in space 4.

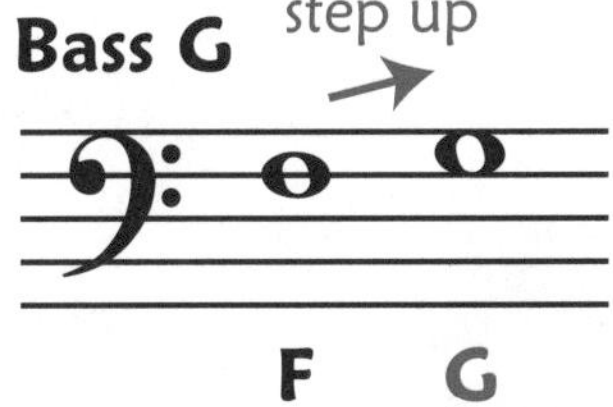

2. Using whole notes, draw Bass G three times.

3. Name the notes.

Lesson Book: page 43

E in Bass Clef

- **Bass E** is a step *down* from Bass F.
- **Bass E** is written in space 3.

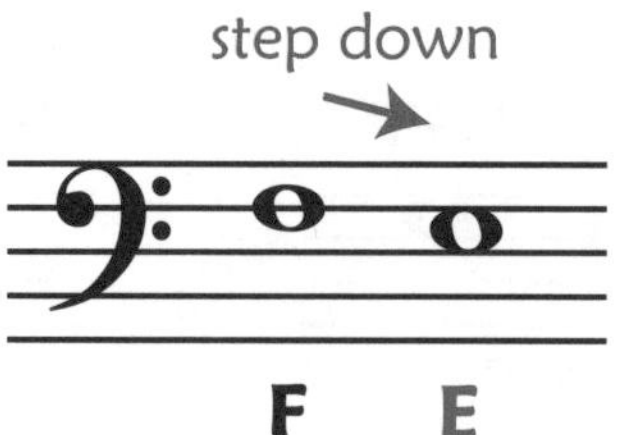

1. Using whole notes, draw Bass E three times.

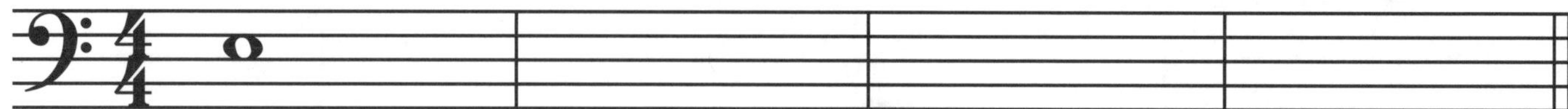

2. Name the notes.

3. Write the letter name on the basketball that is *down* a step and *up* a step from each given letter.

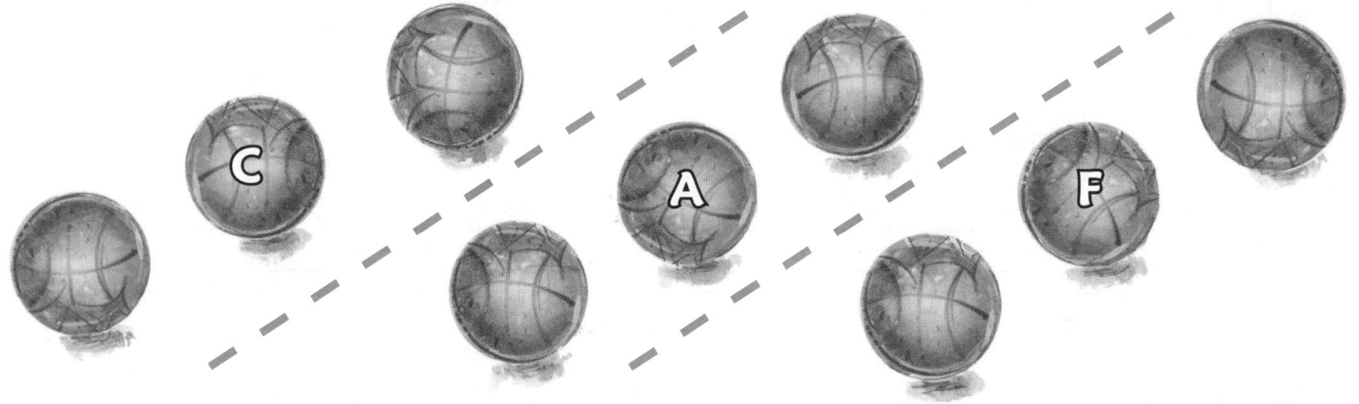

4. A step moves from a line to the next

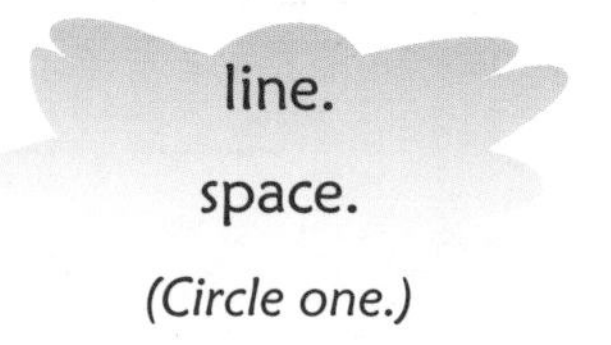

(Circle one.)

5. A step moves from a space to the next

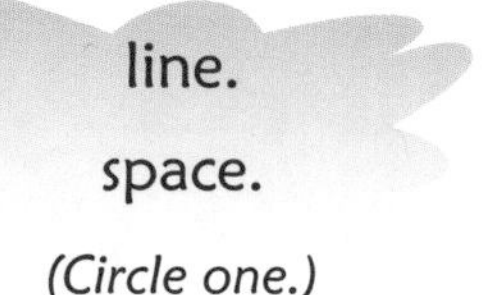

(Circle one.)

Lesson Book: page 44

Bass C and Stem Direction

- **Bass C** is written in space 2.
- **Bass C** is lower than LH Middle C and Bass F.

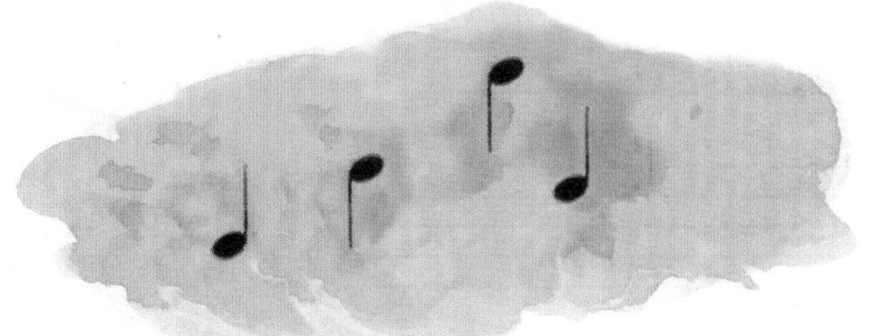

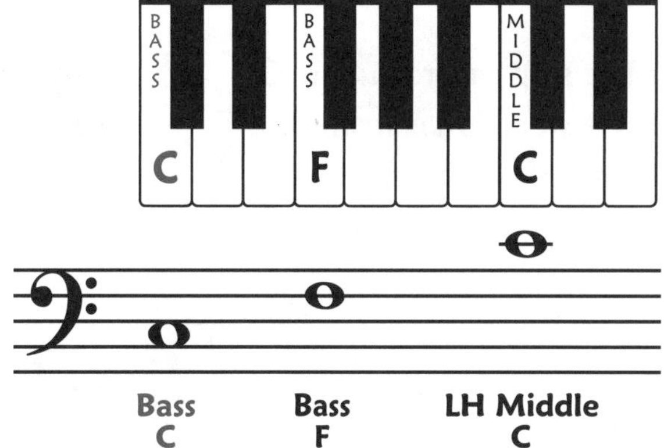

1. Using whole notes, draw Bass C three times.

2. Write the note names.

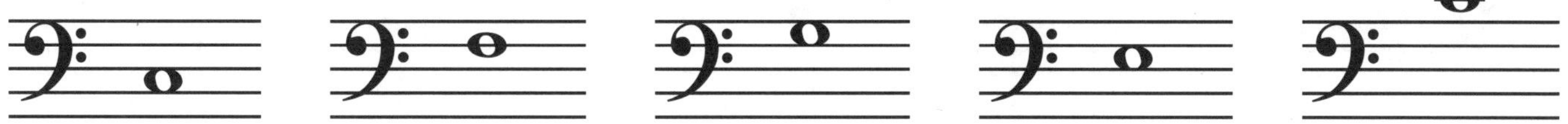

___ ___ ___ ___ ___

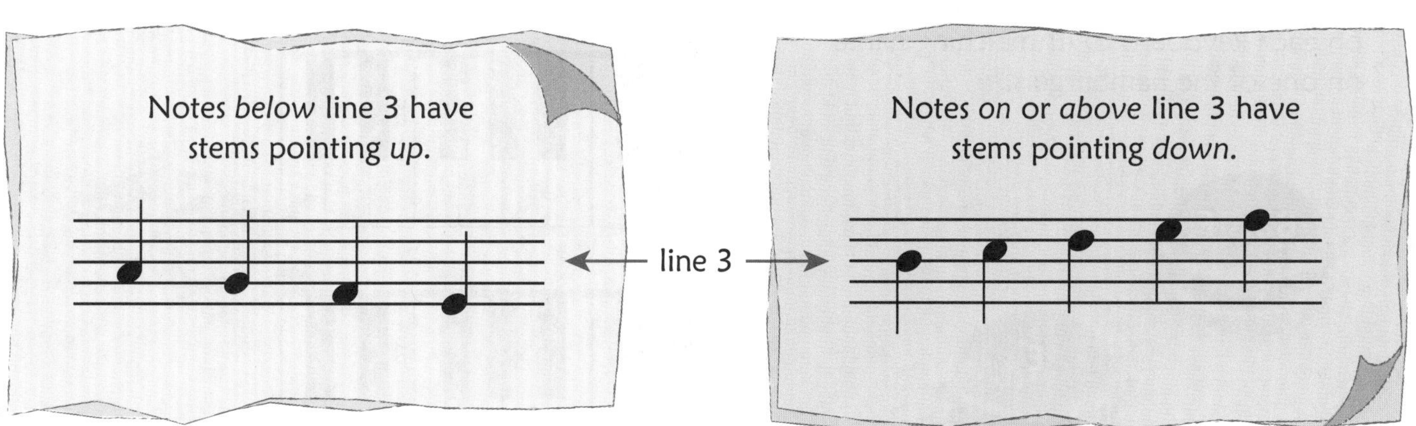

3. On the right side of each notehead, draw a stem pointing *up*.

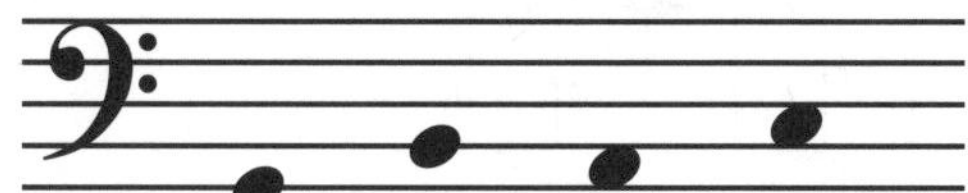

4. On the left side of each notehead, draw a stem pointing *down*.

D in Bass Clef

Lesson Book: page 45

- **Bass D** is a step *up* from Bass C.
- **Bass D** is a step *down* from Bass E.
- **Bass D** is written on line 3.

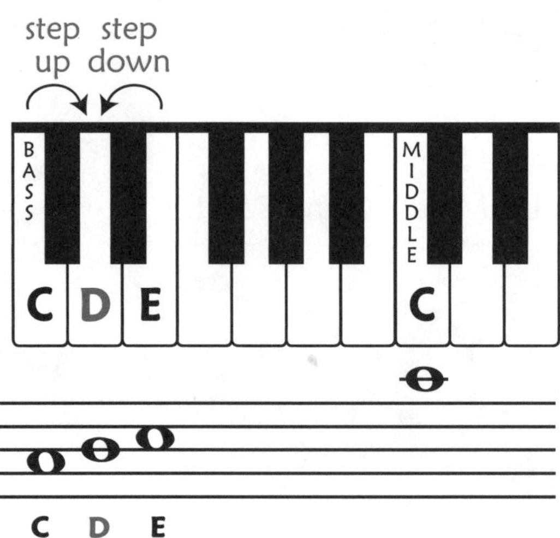

1. Using whole notes, draw Bass D three times.

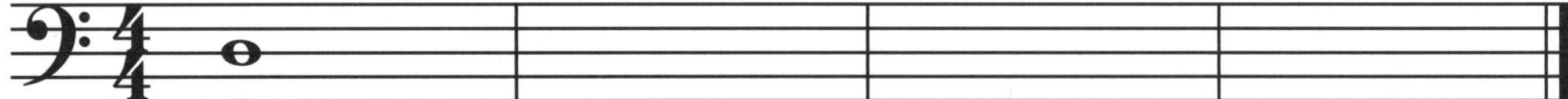

2. Name the notes. Then, play on the keyboard.

3. Draw a line to connect the key marked X on each keyboard to its matching name on one of the hamburgers.

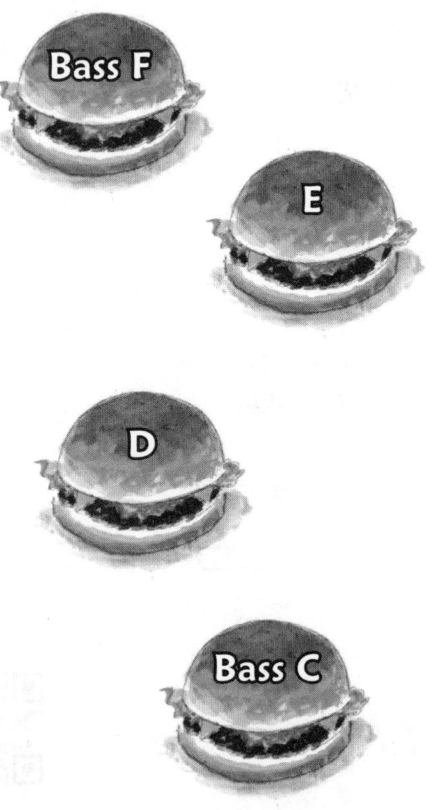

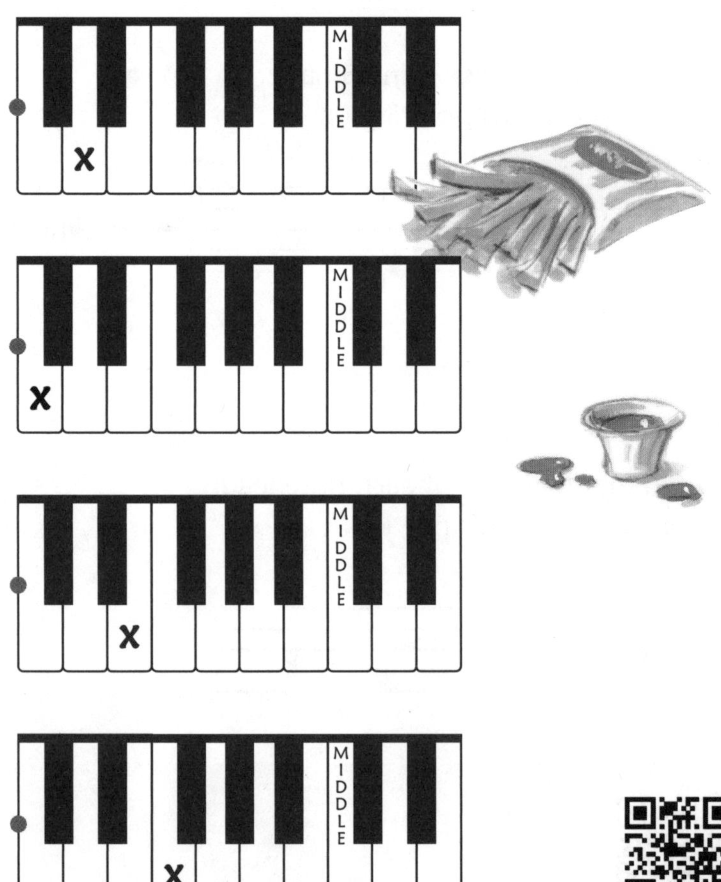

Lesson Book: page 46

C 5-Finger Pattern in Bass Clef

1. Name each note in the C 5-finger pattern in bass clef.

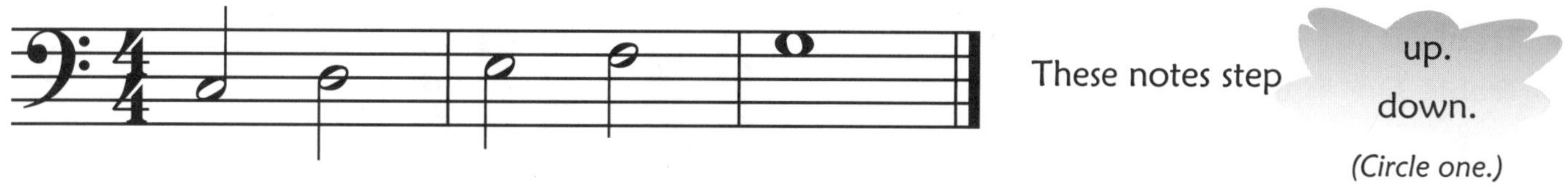

These notes step up. / down.
(Circle one.)

2. Name each note in the C 5-finger pattern in bass clef.

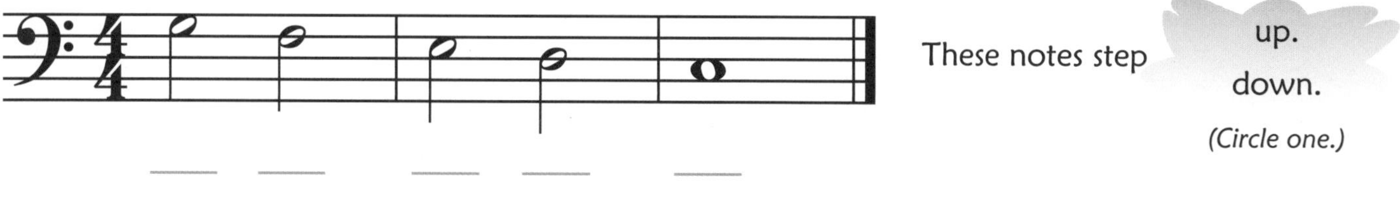

These notes step up. / down.
(Circle one.)

3. Draw a line to connect each note on a T-shirt to its matching name on one of the skateboards.

D G E F C

Lesson Book: page 48

D and E in Treble Clef

- **Treble D** is a step *up* from Middle C.
- **Treble D** is in the space below the staff.
- **Treble E** is a step *up* from Treble D.
- **Treble E** is written on line 1.

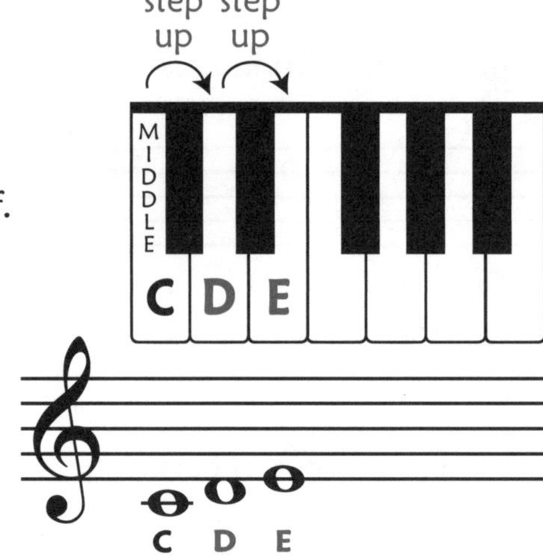

1. Using half notes, draw Treble D and Treble E three times.

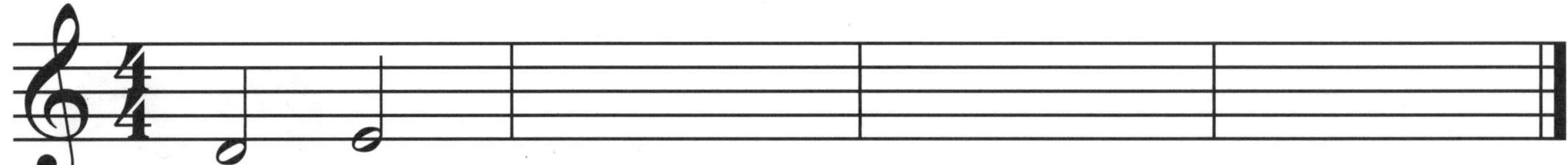

2. Name the notes to learn about this famous composer.

Meet Johann Sebastian Bach (1685–1750)

Ba ___ h was on ___ ___ thrown in jail by his

employ ___ r, a ___ uk ___ ! Whil ___ h ___ was jail ___ ___ ,

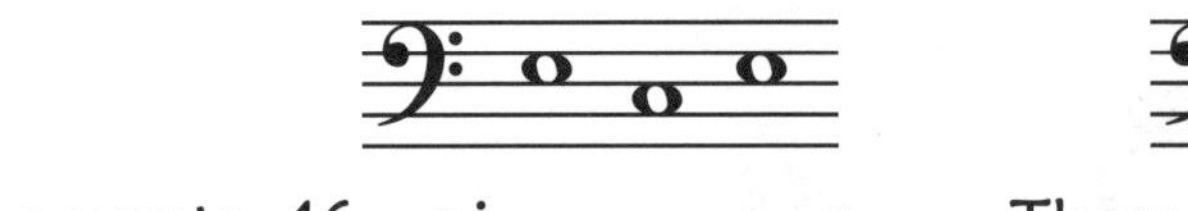

he wrote 46 pi ___ ___ ___ s. These pi ___ ___ ___ s

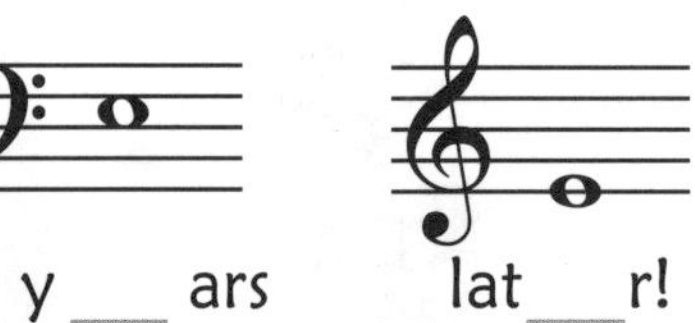

ar ___ still play ___ ___ 300 y ___ ars lat ___ r!

Lesson Book: page 49

F in Treble Clef

- **Treble F** is a step *down* from Treble G.
- **Treble F** is written in space 1.

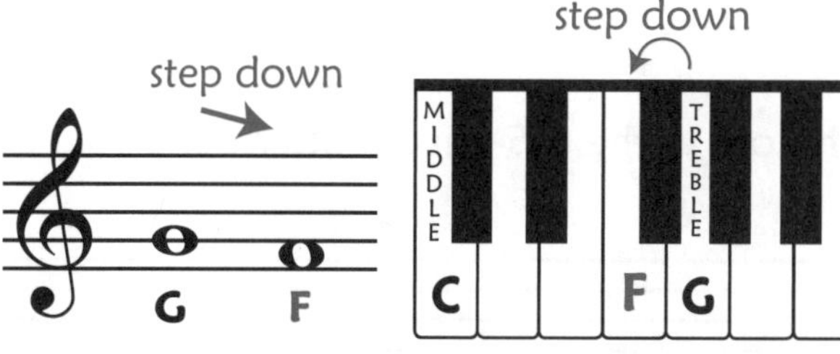

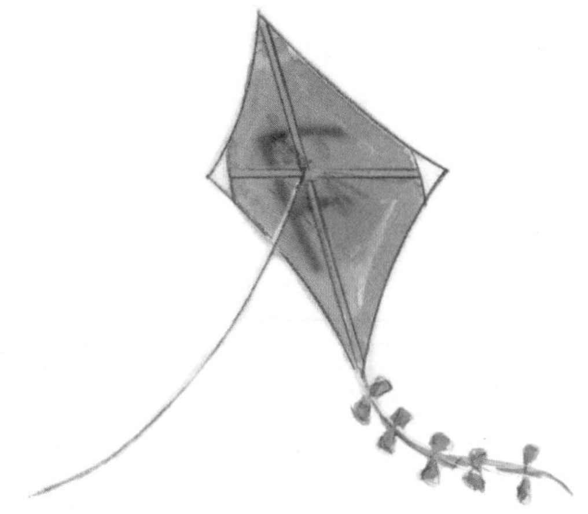

1. Using whole notes, draw Treble F three times.

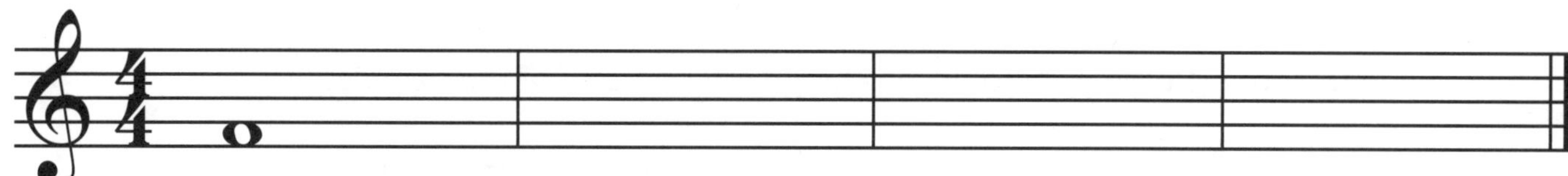

2. Draw a half note that is a step *up* from each note. Draw the stem pointing *up* on the right side of each notehead. Then, name each note.

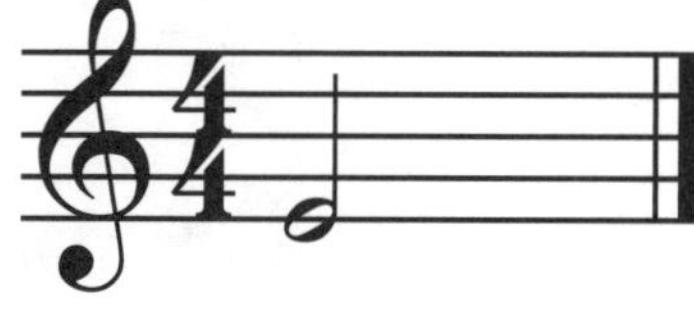

3. Write a half note that is a step *down* from each note. Then, name each note.

Lesson Book: page 50

C 5-Finger Pattern in Treble Clef

1. Name each note in the C 5-finger pattern in treble clef.

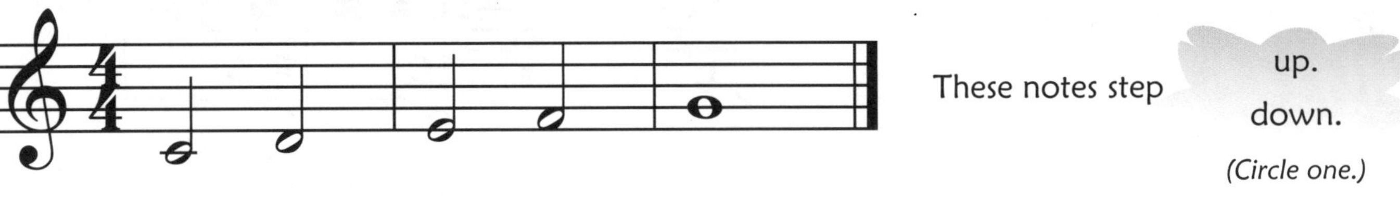

____ ____ ____ ____ ____

These notes step up. / down. *(Circle one.)*

2. Name each note in the C 5-finger pattern in treble clef.

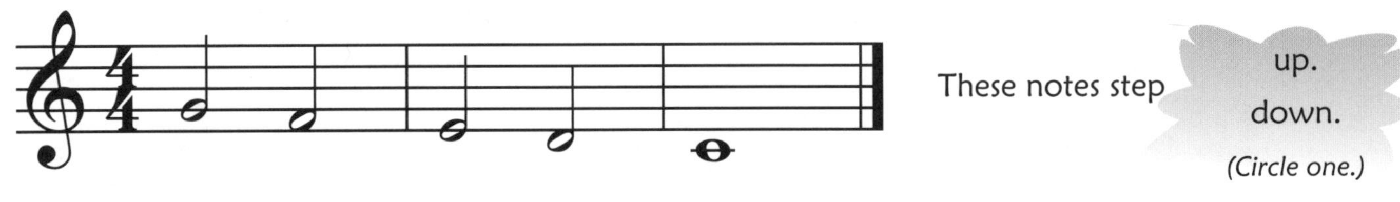

____ ____ ____ ____ ____

These notes step up. / down. *(Circle one.)*

3. Draw a line to connect each note to its matching name on one of the trophies.

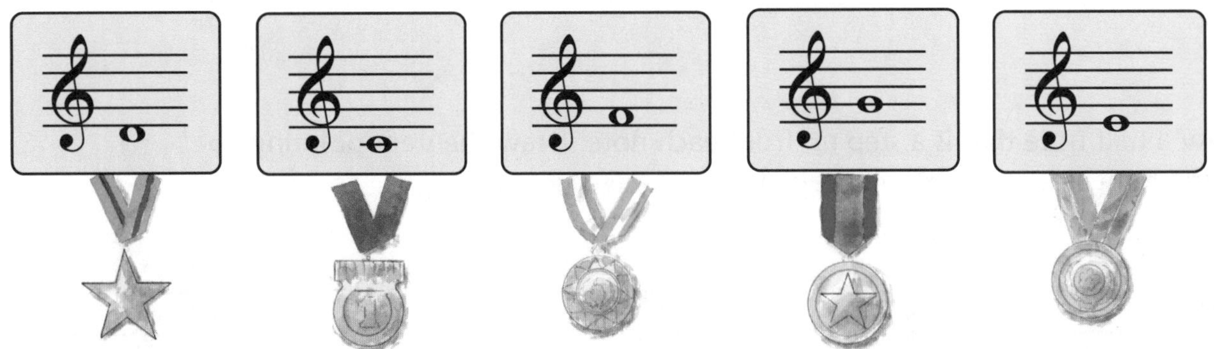

Lesson Book: page 51

More About the C 5-Finger Pattern

1. Name the notes to learn about this famous composer.

Meet Ludwig van Beethoven (1770–1827)

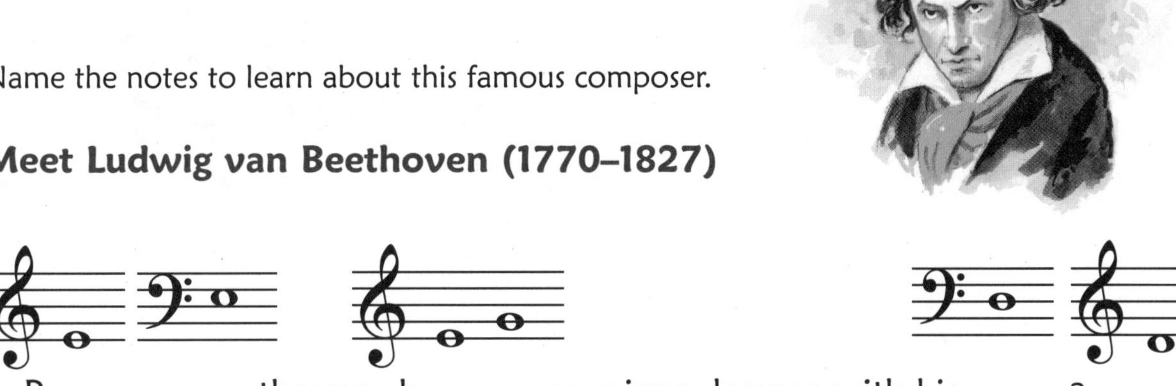

B___ ___thoven b___ ___an piano lessons with his ___ a ___

wh___n h___ was ___our y___ars ol___.

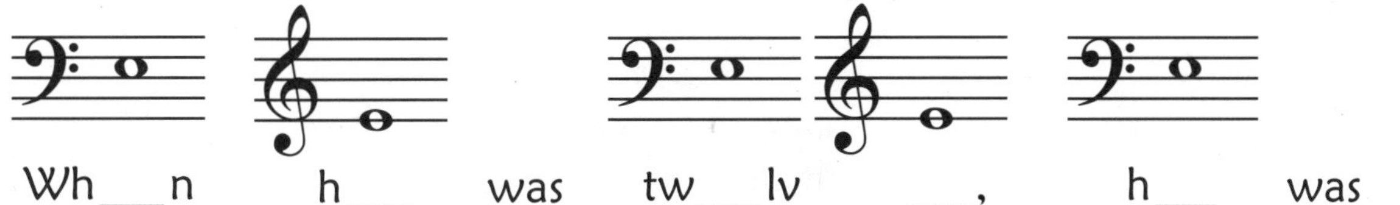

Wh___n h___ was tw___lv___, h___ was

a ___ourt or___anist. His salary support___ ___

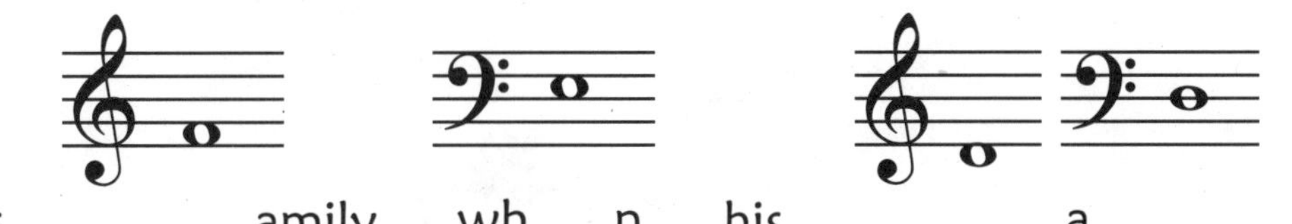

his ___amily wh___n his ___ a ___ could not.

2. Name the notes. Then, play on the keyboard.

Lesson Book: page 53

B and A in Bass Clef

- **B** is a step *down* from Middle C.
- **B** is written in the space above the staff.
- **A** is a step *down* from B.
- **A** is written on line 5.

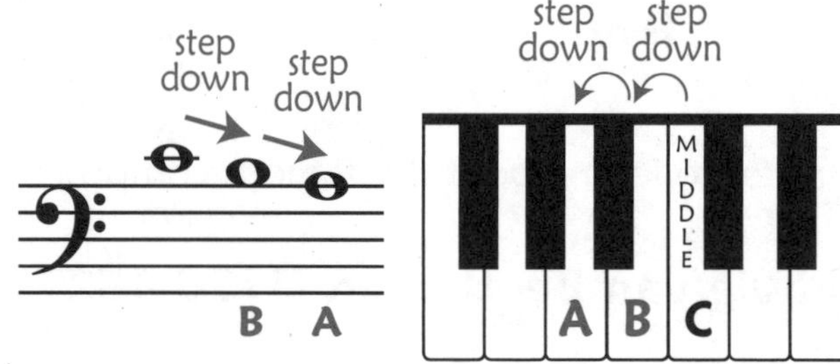

1. Using half notes, draw B and A three times.

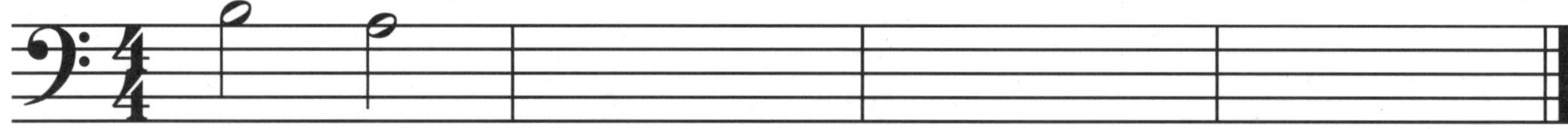

2. Draw a line to connect each note to its matching name on one of the snowballs.

A

G

B

F

C

Lesson Book: page 54

Stepping Down from Middle C to Bass F

1. Name each note in this bass staff 5-finger pattern.

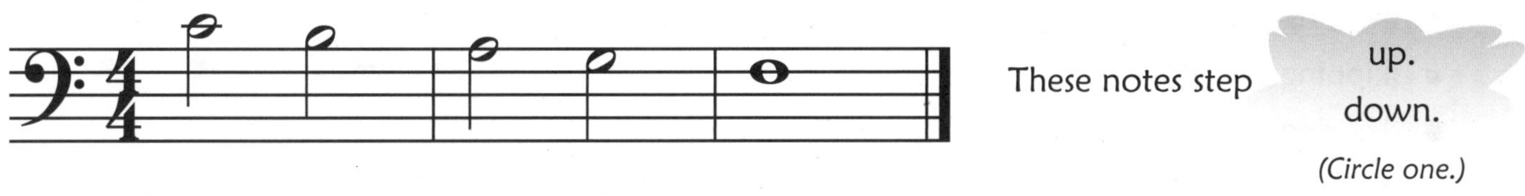

___ ___ ___ ___ ___

2. Name each note in this bass staff 5-finger pattern.

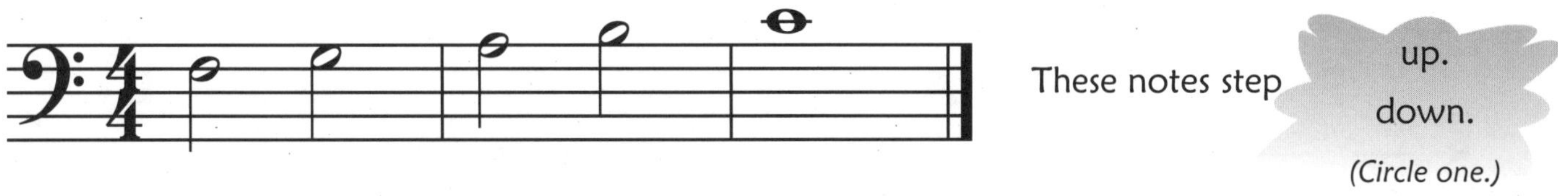

___ ___ ___ ___ ___

3. Name the notes. Then, play on the keyboard.

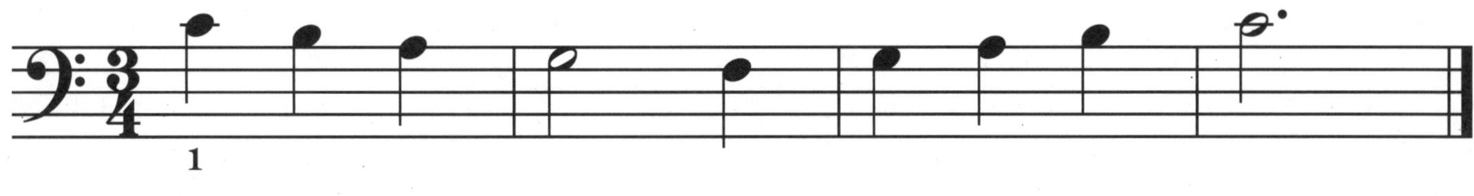

___ ___ ___ ___ ___ ___ ___ ___ ___

4. Draw a half note that is a step *up* from each note. Draw the stem pointing *down* on the left side of each notehead. Then, name each note.

___ ___ ___ ___ ___ ___

5. Draw a half note that is a step *down* from each note. Then, name each note.

___ ___ ___ ___ ___ ___

Lesson Book: page 56

Skip

A skip moves up or down:

- skipping a **white key**.
- skipping a **finger**.
- skipping a **letter**.

1. Write the letter names that are *up* and *down* a skip from each given letter.

2. Write the number above the finger that is *up* a skip from each given finger number.

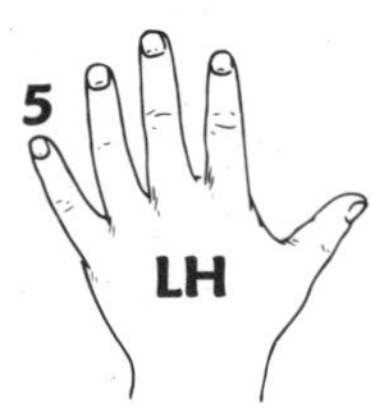

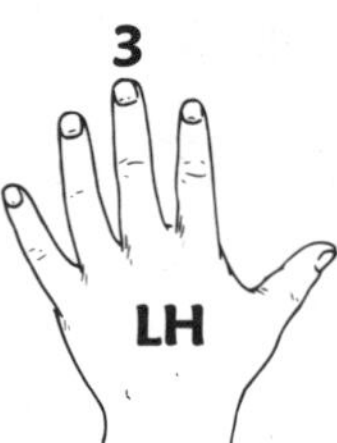

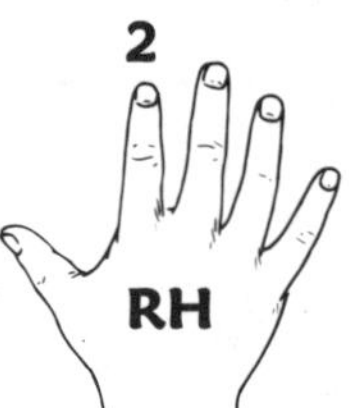

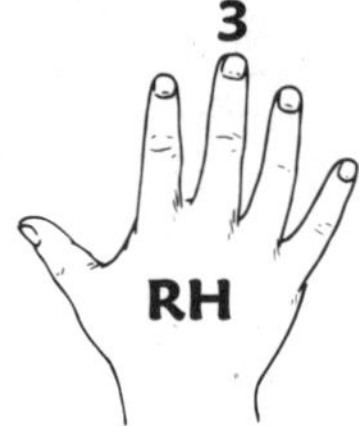

3. Write the number above the finger that is *down* a skip from each given finger number.

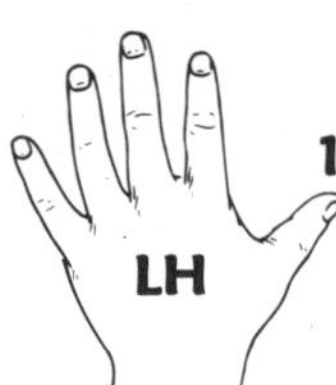

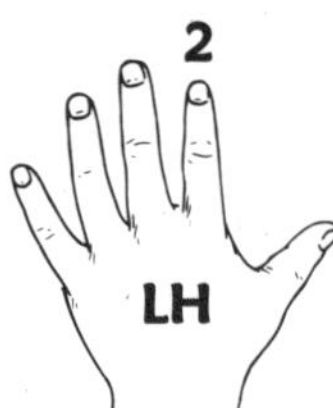

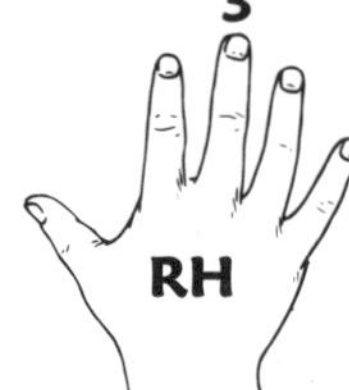

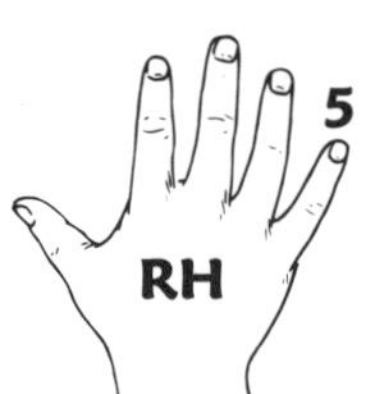

4. Write the letter name on the key that is *up* a skip from each key marked X.

5. Write the letter name on the key that is *down* a skip from each key marked X.

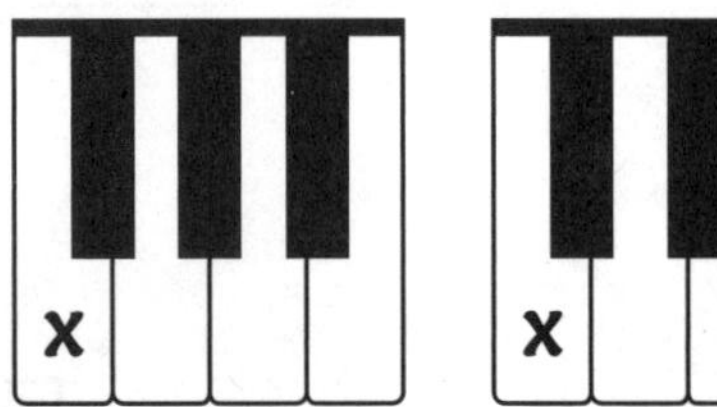

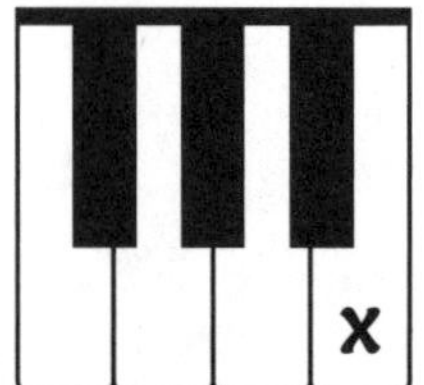

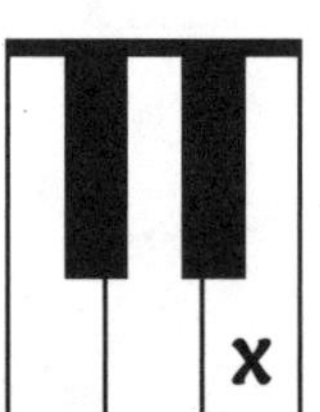

Lesson Book: pages 56–57

Skips on the Staff

On the staff, a skip moves *up* or *down*, line to line or space to space.

Skipping up

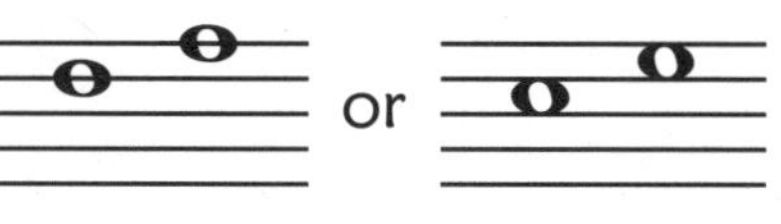

line to line space to space

Skipping down

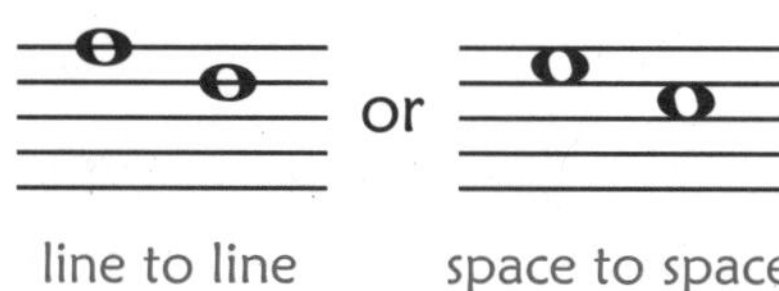

line to line space to space

1. Draw a line to connect each *skip* on the staff to the alarm clock that describes how it moves.

2. Draw a half note that is a skip *up* from each note. Draw the stem pointing *up* on the right side of each notehead. Then, name each note.

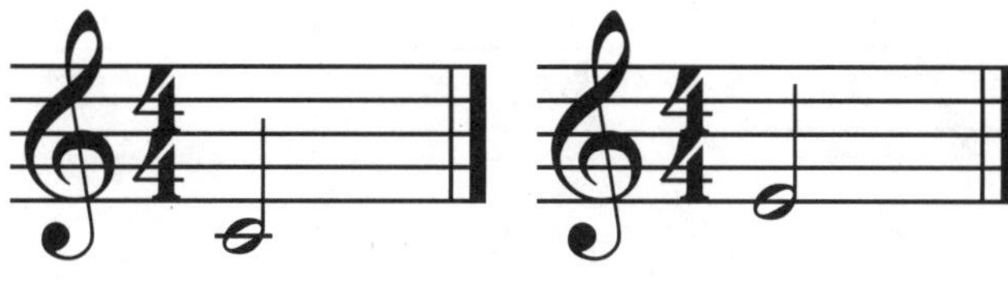

3. Draw a half note that is a skip *down* from each note. Draw the stem pointing *down* on the left side of each notehead. Then, name each note.

More About Skips

Lesson Book: page 60

1. A skip moves from a space to a space. / line. *(Circle one.)*

2. A skip moves from a line to a space. / line. *(Circle one.)*

3. Circle *step* or *skip* for each example.

4. Name the notes to learn about this famous composer.

Meet Wolfgang Amadeus Mozart (1756–1791)

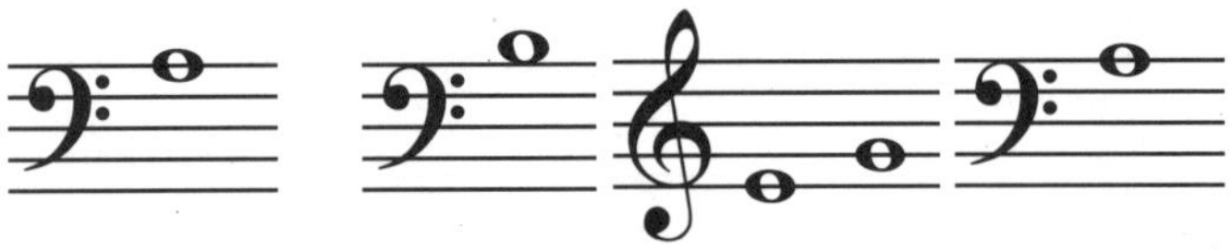

Moz__rt __ __ __ __n

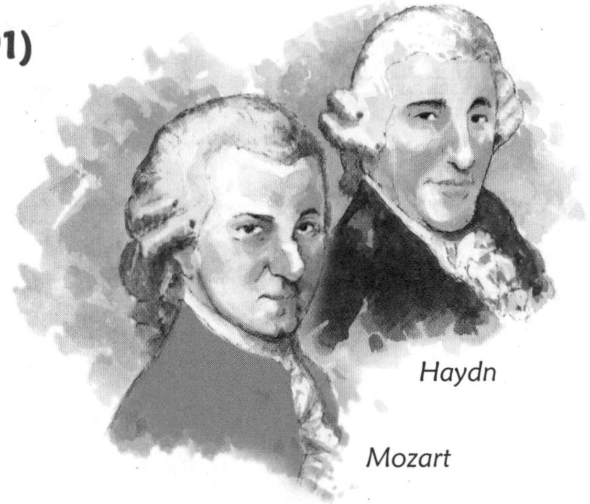

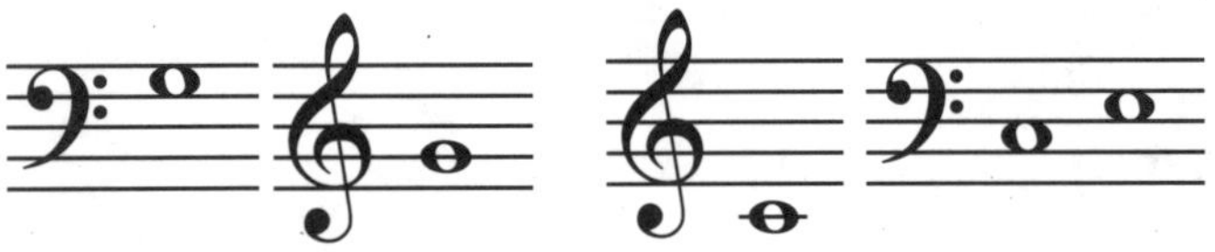

__ivin __ __ on __ __rts

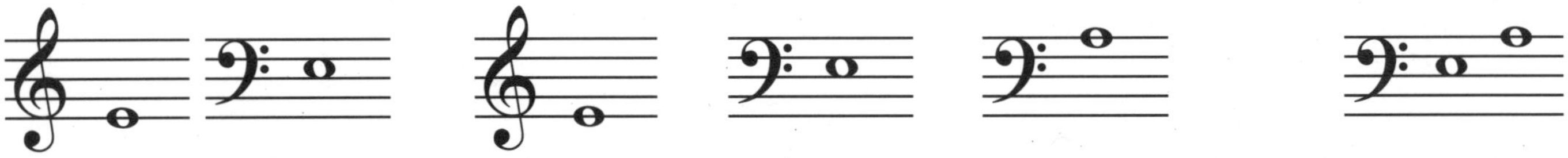

in __urop __ wh__n h__ w__s just six y__ __rs

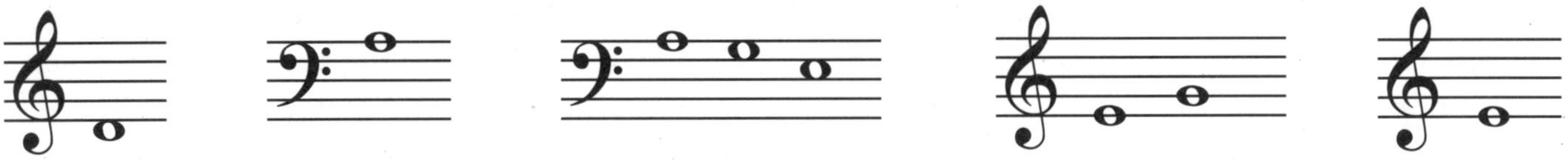

ol__! __t __ __ __ __i__ht, h__

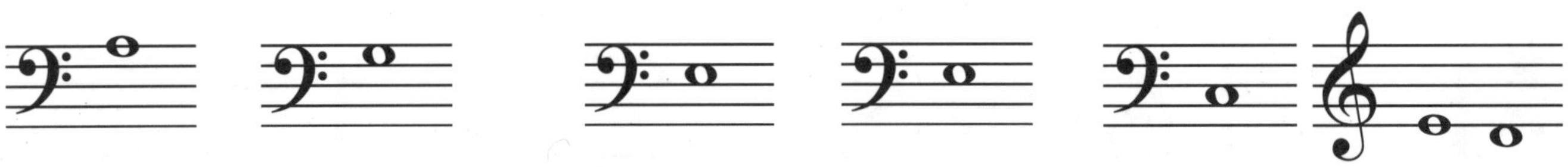

w__s writin__ symphoni__s. H__ __ompos__ __ his

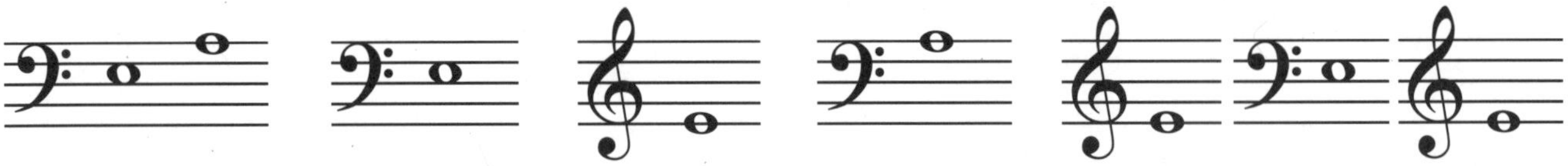

first op__r__ wh__n h__ w__s __ l __ v __n!

Haydn

Mozart

Steps and Skips

Lesson Book: page 61

1. Name the notes. Then, circle *steps* or *skips* for each example.

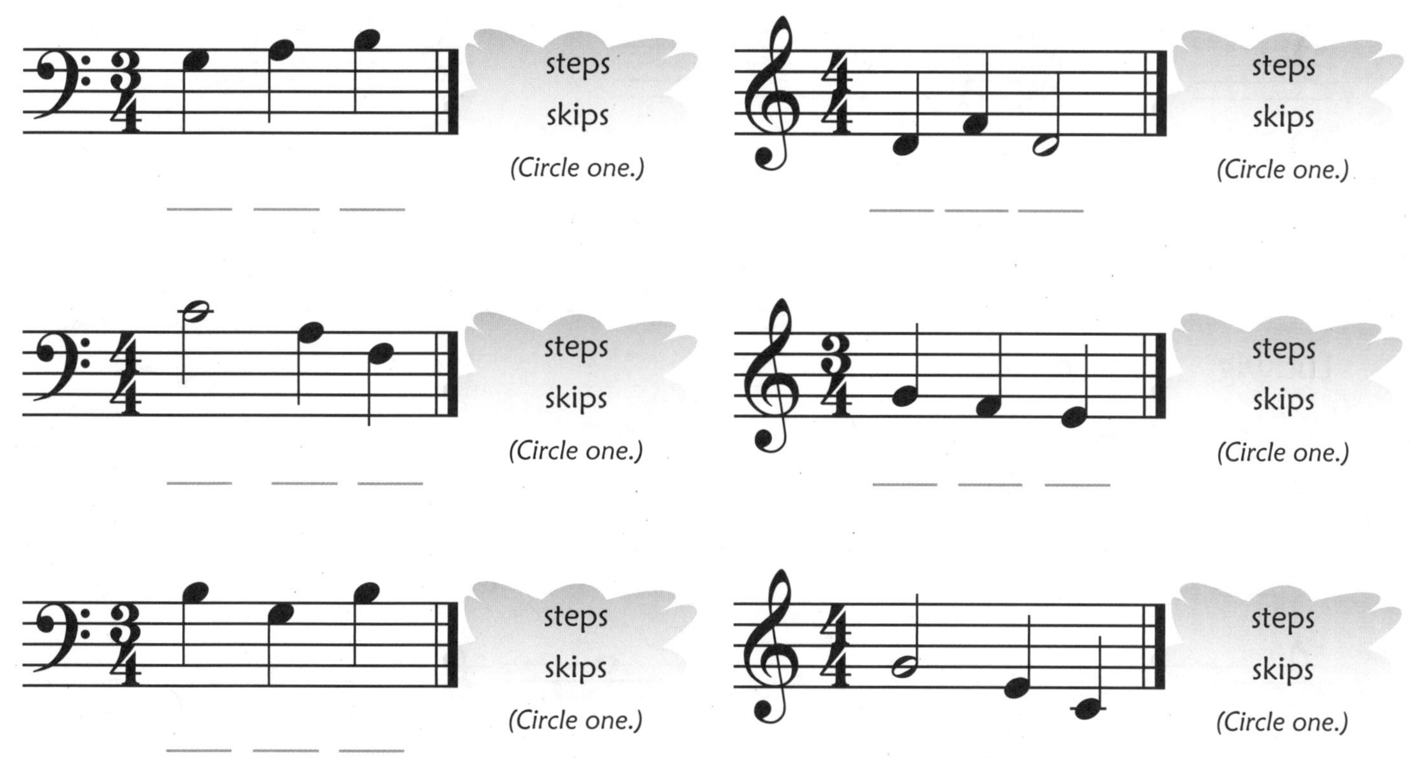

2. Name the notes to learn about this famous composer.

Meet Franz Joseph Haydn (1732–1809)

Review

Lesson Book: pages 62–63

1. Name the notes to discover the composers whose music was on the recital program.

Joh___nn S___ ___ ___sti___n ___ ___ ___h

Ludwig v___n ___ ___ ___ thov___n

Fr___nz Jos___ph H___y___n

Wol___ ___ ___n___ ___m___ ___ ___us Moz___rt

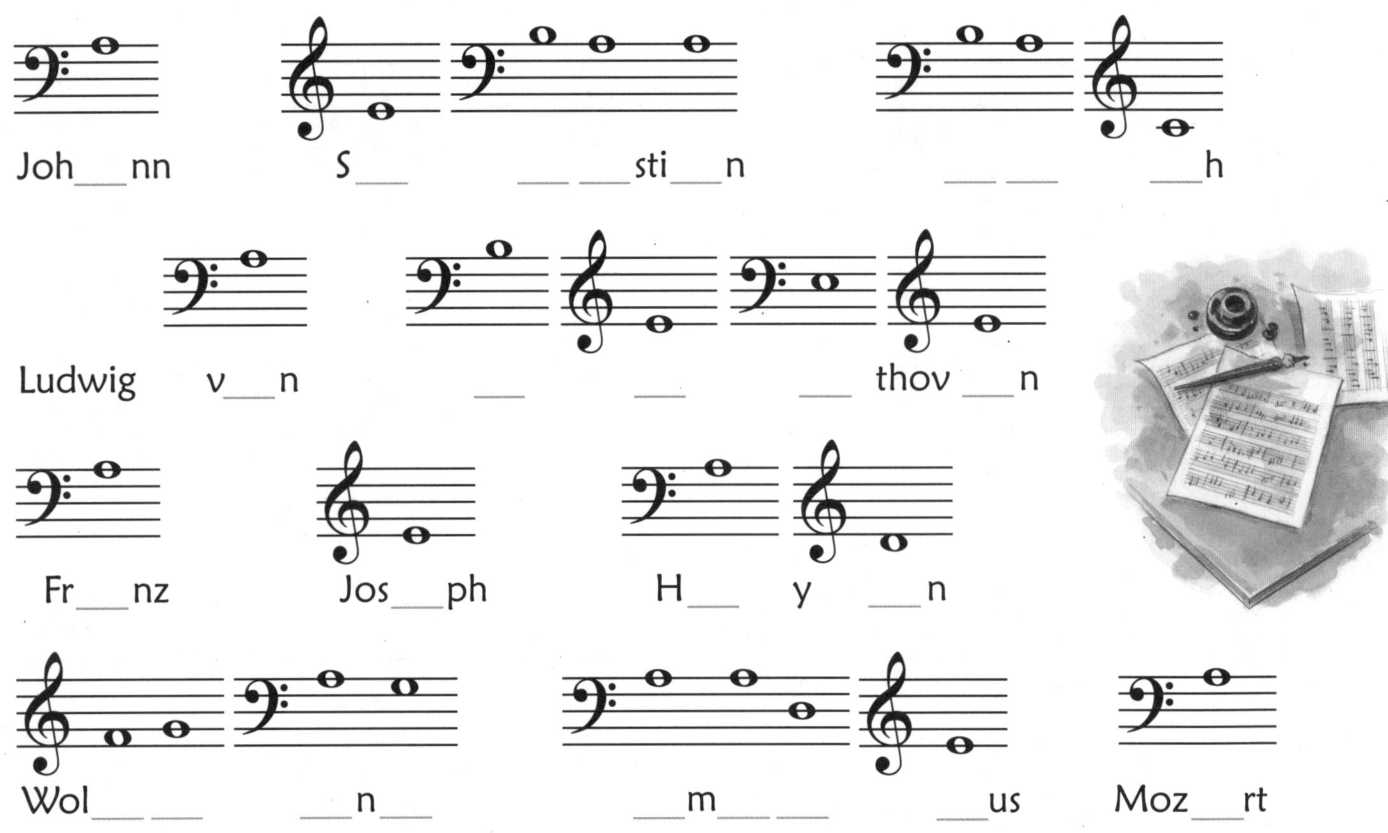

2. Draw a line to connect the notes on the staff to their names on one of the piano benches.

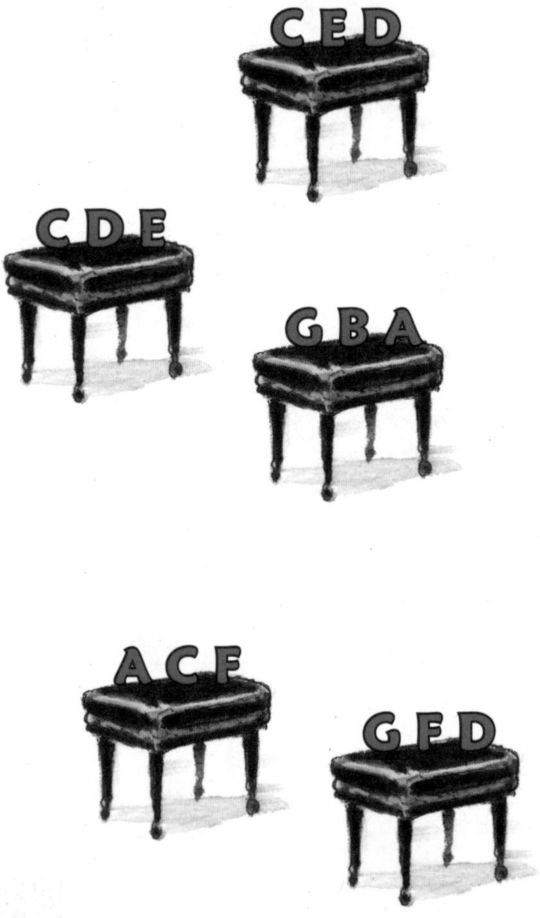
CED
CDE
GBA
ACF
GFD

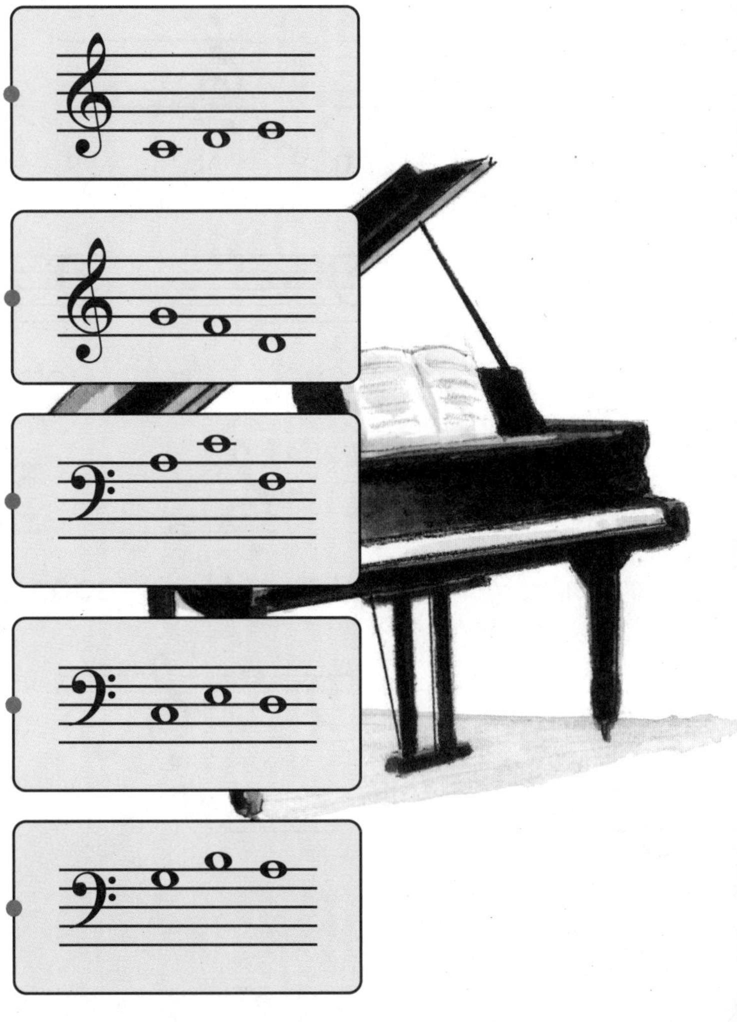